كتــاب المـــوت

THE BOOK OF DEATH

By

Sheikh Faisal Abdur-Razak

Published By

Al-Attique Publishers Inc, Canada

Title :   **THE BOOK OF DEATH**
Copyright: All rights reserved
Printed :   1999
Printing supervised by :   M.R. Attique

© Al-Attique Publishers Inc, CANADA 1999
ISBN + CIP National Library of Canada
1-894264-05-3

Published by:
Al-Attique Publishers Inc, Canada
65 Treverton Drive, Scarborough
Ontario M1K 3S5 Canada
Tel: (416) 615-1222   Fax: (416) 615-0375
E-mail: quran@istar.ca
Website: http://home.istar.ca/~quran

In the name of Allah, the Most Gracious, the Most Merciful.

﴿ كُلُّ نَفْسٍ ذَائِقَةُ الْمَوْتِ وَإِنَّمَا تُوَفَّوْنَ أُجُورَكُمْ يَوْمَ الْقِيَامَةِ فَمَنْ زُحْزِحَ عَنِ النَّارِ وَأُدْخِلَ الْجَنَّةَ فَقَدْ فَازَ وَمَا الْحَيَاةُ الدُّنْيَا إِلَّا مَتَاعُ الْغُرُورِ ﴾

Everyone shall taste death. And only on the Day of Resurrection shall you be paid your wages in full. And whoever is removed away from the Fire and admitted to Paradise, he indeed is successful. The life of this world is only the enjoyment of deception (adeceiving thing). [3-185]

DEDICATION

TO

AL-SHAHEED AHMAD IBRAHIM EHWAAS

FOR

MAKING THE ULTIMATE SACRIFICE : LIVING AND DYING FOR THE PLEASURE OF ALLAH

﴿ وَلَا تَحْسَبَنَّ الَّذِيْنَ قُتِلُوا فِي سَبِيْلِ اللهِ أَمْوَاتاً بَلْ أَحْيَاءٌ عِنْدَ رَبِّهِمْ يُرْزَقُوْنَ ﴾

" Think not of those who are killed in the way
of Allah
as dead. nay, they are alive, with their lord,
and they have to provision.
[SURAH AALI-'IMRAAN, 3:169]

4

TABLE OF CONTENTS

Page

5

6

PUBLISHER'S NOTE

Al-Attique Publishers Inc. Canada feel pleasure to publish " **THE BOOK OF DEATH**" by Br. Faisal Abdur Razaq.

Sheikh Faisal Abdur Razaq is the Immam of Tarik masjid Toronto and prominent scholar of North America. He is serving the Muslim community since he completed his education from Umm-UL-Qura University Makkah tul Mukarama. He is very dedicated for Islam and spending his day and nights in the field of Da'awa. He has written several books. it is very pleasure for our establishment that he authorized us to publish his work. This book Kitab Al-Mawt is very important for every Muslim. One should obligatory know about Islamic etiquettes of sickness and consoling the sick person and his family members, supplication for sick or dying person, importance of making a will in sickness, obligation to the dead person, funeral prayers, burial procedure and debts of deceased etc..

Shiekh Faisal completed this important job very successfully for the Muslim community particularly for north American Muslims, and gave good guidance in simple and proper way. We pray form Allah (swt) to give him further (Taufeeq) to serve human beings and put his struggle in his Hasanat in the hereafter. A'amin.

Your Brother in Islam
M.R. Attique
The Publisher, Canada.
Nov, 01, 1998.

INTRODUCTION

I seek refuge in Almighty Allah from Satan, the rejected one. And I begin in the Name of Allah, who is Most Gracious and Most Merciful. All Praise is due to Allah, the Cherisher and Sustainer of the entire Universe. Most Gracious, Most Merciful. Master of the Day of Judgement. You alone we worship, and to You alone we pray for help. Guide us on the Straight Path. The path of those on whom You Have bestowed your Grace, Those whose portion is not wrath, And who go not astray.

This book comprises of three sections as follows:

PART 1 : ETIQUETTES RELATING TO SICKNESS AND DEATH

PART 2 : JANAAZAH AND RELATED MATTERS.

PART 3 : PHASES OF EXISTENCE.

In Part 1, the topics dealt with include importance of visiting the sick, supplication for the sick, consoling the sick person, encouraging the dying person to pronounce the Shahaadah, saying good words before a dying person and his relatives, supplication or Du'aa to be recited after a person dies, excellence of participation in the funeral prayers, burial as soon as possible after death, speedy payment of the debts of the deceased, and charity on behalf of the deceased.

In Part 2, Janaazah and related matters are discussed. The topics include the importance of making a will (Wasiyyah), what to do when a person is on the verge of dying, our obligations to the dead person, bathing the corpse or Ghusl, shrouding the corpse or kafan, the funeral prayer or Salaatul Janaazah, and the burial or Dafn.

In Part 3, the Phases of Existence are discussed. The topics covered are the four phases of existence : life in the womb, life on earth, life in the grave, and life in the hereafter. Also included are some reflections about the journey of life. It is hoped that this book will be useful to all those who read it.

Above all, I am eternally grateful to Almighty Allah (SWT), for the accomplishment of this work.

WMA TOUFIQI ILLA BILLA

Faisal Abu Jehad , Toronto , Canada.

PART-I

ETIQUETTES RELATING TO SICKNESS AND DEATH

CHAPTER - 1

IMPORTANCE OF VISITING THE SICK

1.   Bara' Ibn 'Aazib (May Allah be pleased with him) narrated: The Messenger of Allah ﷺ has ordered us to pay a visit to the sick, to follow the funeral processions, to respond to the sneezer, to help the oppressed, to accept the invitation extended by the inviter; and to respond to the salutations. (Agreed upon)

2.   Abu Hurayrah (May Allah be pleased with him) reported that the Messenger of Allah ﷺ said: Every Muslim has five duties to perform for another Muslim: to return the greetings, to visit the sick, to accompany funeral processions, to accept an invitation, to give response to the sneezer (Say: May Allah bestow His mercy on you when the sneezer praises Allah). (Agreed upon)

3.   Abu Hurayrah (May Allah be pleased with

him) reported that the Messenger of Allah ﷺ said: Verily, Allah, the Exalted and Glorious would say on the Day of Resurrection: O son of Adam, I was indisposed but you did not pay a visit to Me. He would say: O my Lord, how could I pay a visit to you because You are the Lord of the Universe? Thereupon He would say: Did not you know that such and such servant of Mine was ailing but you did not visit him. Behold! you must be fully aware (ofthis fact) if you had visited him, you would have found Me there. O son of Adam, I asked food from you but you did not feed Me. He would submit: My Lord, how could I feed You and You are the Lord of the worlds? He said: Did not you remember that such and such servant of Mine begged food from you but you declined to feed him. You must be aware (of this fact) that if you had fed him, you would have found its reward from Me. (The Lord would again say): O son of Adam, I asked water from you but you did not give it to Me. He would say: My Lord, how could I provide You (water) and You are the Lord of the worlds? Thereupon He would say: Such and such of

My servants asked you for water to drink but you did not provide him with water. Behold! You must be aware (of this fact) that had you provided him (with water), you would have found its reward from Me. (Muslim)

4. Abu Musa (May Allah be pleased with him) reported that the Messenger of Allah. ﷺ said: Visit the sick, feed the hungry, and release the captive. (Bukhari)

5. Thauban (May Allah be pleased with him) reported that the Messenger of Allah ﷺ said: He who inquires after the health of his brother in faith, is supposed to remain engaged in picking the fruit from the garden of Paradise till he returns. It was asked: O'Allah's Messenger! what is Khurfat-ul-Jannah? He replied: It means picking of fruit from the place where fruit is found in abundance. (Muslim)

6. 'Ali (May Allah be pleased with him) reported that he heard the Messenger of Allah ﷺ saying: When a Muslim inquires after the health of another sick Muslim at dawn, seventy thousand angels continue seeking

salvation for him till dusk. If he visits him in the evening seventy thousand angels continue invoking blessings on him till the morning and he will have gathered fruit in Paradise. (Tirmidhi)

7. Anas (May Allah be pleased with him) narrated: A young Jewish boy who rendered services to the Messenger of Allah ﷺ became ill. The Apostle of Allah ﷺ went to visit him. He sat down by his head and said to him: Embrace Islam. He glanced at his father who was sitting beside him, and his father said: Obey Abul Qasim. So the young boy embraced Islam and the Messenger of Allah ﷺ stepped out saying: Praise be to Allah Who has saved him from Hell. (Bukhari)

CHAPTER 2
SUPPLICATION FOR THE SICK

2.1 'A'isha (May Allah be pleased with her) reported: Whenever a person complained to the Messenger of Allah ﷺ about an ailment, or suffered from a sore or a wound, the Messenger of Allah ﷺ used to touch the ground with his forefinger and then lift it and recite: "In the name of Allah, the dust of our ground mixed with the saliva of any one of us would serve as a means whereby the illness of our patient would be cured with the sanction of our Lord." (Agreed upon)

2.2 'A'isha (May Allah be pleased with her) reported: When the Messenger of Allah ﷺ visited any member of his family he used to touch the invalid with his right hand and beseech: "O Allah! Lord of mankind! Remove this disease and cure him! You are the Great Curer. There is no cure but through Your healing power which leaves behind no disease." (Agreed upon)

2.3 Anas (May Allah be pleased with him)

reported: He said to Thabit (Allah be pleased with him): Should I not pray over you such supplication as was practised by the Messenger of Allah ﷺ? He said: Please do so. Anas (Allah be pleased with him) supplicated: O' Allah! Lord of the people! Take away this disease and cure him. You are the Curer. There is no curer except You. There is no cure but through Your healing power, a cure that leaves no disease. (Bukhari)

2.4 Sa'd bin Abi Waqqas (Allah be pleased with him) reported: The Messenger of Allah ﷺ visited him during his illness and prayed: "O' Allah! Cure Sa'd, O' Allah! Cure Sa'd, O' Allah! Cure Sa'd." (Muslim)

2.5 Abu 'Abdullah 'Uthman bin Abi al-'Aas (May Allah be pleased with him) reported: He complained to the Messenger of Allah ﷺ about his disease. Thereupon the Apostle of Allah ﷺ said: Place your hand at the part of your body, where you feel pain and say: Bismillah (in the name of Allah) three times; and then repeat seven times: I seek refuge with Allah and with His power from the evil that afflicts me and that I apprehend. (Muslim)

2.6 Ibn Abbas (May Allah be pleased with him) reported that the Messenger of Allah ﷺ said: If a person inquires about the health of such an invalid person as is not on the point of death and supplicates seven times: I beseech Allah the Glorious, Lord of the Glorious Throne, to cure your disease; Allah will relieve him of his sickness. (Abu Dawud and Tirmidhi)

2.7 Ibn 'Abbas (May Allah be pleased with him) reported: The Messenger of Allah ﷺ visited a rustic who was ailing. Whenever he visited an invalid he used to say: "Have no fear. The ailment will prove itself purifying, if Allah wills." (Bukhari)

2.8 Abu Sa'id al-Khudri (May Allah be pleased with him) reported that Jibra'il عليه السلام came to the Messenger of Allah ﷺ and said: O' Muhammad! Are you indisposed? He replied in the affirmative. Jibra'il said: I exorcise you from all that troubles you and safeguard you from every harmful mischief and from the eyes of a jealous one. Allah will cure you and I invoke the name of Allah for you. (Muslim)

2.9 Abu Said Khudri and Abu Huraira (May Allah be pleased with them both) report and bear testimony in respect of the Messenger of Allah ﷺ who said: If a person says: There is none worthy of worship except Allah, the Great, his Lord responds to him and affirms: There is none worthy of worship except I, and I am the Great. When he says: There is none worthy of worship except Allah, the One, He has no partner. He (Allah) affirms: There is none worthy of worship except I alone. I have no partner. When he says: There is none worthy of worship except Allah, The Sovereignty belongs to Him and all the praise is due to Him; He affirms: There is none worthy of worship save I, Mine is the praise and Mine is the sovereignty. When he says: There is none worthy of worship except Allah, and there is no might and power but with Allah, He affirms: There is none worthy of worship save I, and there is no might and power but that of Allah. The Messenger of Allah ﷺ added: He who utters this during his illness and dies, will not be consumed by the Fire of Hell. (Tirmidhi).

CHAPTER 3

INQUIRING FROM FAMILY MEMBERS
ABOUT THE PATIENT

3.1 Ibn 'Abbas (Allah be pleased with him)
reported: When 'Ali (Allah be pleased with
him) came out after visiting the Messenger
of Allah ﷺ during the fatal illness which
resulted in his demise, the people asked:
How is Allah's Messenger ﷺ, Abul Hasan?
He replied: Praise be to Allah, he is feeling
better. (Reported by Imam Al-Bukhari)

It is very important that we show some interest
in the well being of others when they are sick;
that we find out from their relatives how they are
doing. It is not difficult for us to call them by
telephone if we cannot find the time to visit
them. This is the least we should do.

CHAPTER 4

SUPPLICATION WHEN ONE IS DISAPPOINTED ABOUT ONE'S LIFE

4.1 'A'isha (May Allah be pleased with her) reported: While the Messenger of Allah ﷺ was reclining against her, she heard him saying: O' Allah! Excuse me and bestow Your Mercy me and let me join with the elevated companions. (Bukhari)

4.2 'A'isha (May Allah be pleased with her) reported: I saw the Messenger of Allah ﷺ while he was dying. He had a cup containing water. He would put his hand into the cup, and wipe his face. Then he supplicated: O' Allah! Help me to bear the pain and agony of death. (Tirmidhi)

CHAPTER 5

CONSOLING THE PATIENTS AND SHOWING KINDNESS TO ONE FACINGDEATH SENTENCE

5.1   Imran bin Husain (May Allah be pleased with him) reported: A woman belonging to the Juhaina tribe came to Allah's Messenger ﷺ and she had become pregnant as a result of fornication. She submitted: O' Messenger of Allah! ﷺ I have done something for which punishment must be imposed upon me, so impose that. Allah's Messenger ﷺ called her guardian and said: Treat her well and bring her to me after delivery. He acted accordingly. Then Allah's Messenger ﷺ commanded to tie her clothes firmly around her and then stone her to death. He then offered her funeral prayer. (MUSLIM)

CHAPTER 6

PERMISSIBILITY OF EXPRESSING SOME WORDS IN SERIOUS ILLNESS

6.1 Ibn Mas'ud (May Allah be pleased with him) narrated: I visited the Messenger of Allah ﷺ while he was suffering from a high fever. I said: O Allah's Messenger! You have a high fever. He said, "Yes, I have as high fever as two men of you." (Agreed upon)

6.2 Sa'd bin Abi Waqqas (May Allah be pleased with him) narrated: The Messenger of Allah ﷺ came to visit me when I had a severe pain. I submitted: I am suffering from such trouble as you are observing. I am a wealthy man and the only heir of mine is my daughter. (Agreed upon)

6.3 Qasim bin Muhammad (May Allah be pleased with him) reported that 'A'isha (Allah be pleased with her) said: Oh, my head (It was estranging due to pain); whereupon the Messenger of Allah ﷺ directed her to utter: Oh, my headache. (Bukhari)

CHAPTER 7

ENCOURAGING THE DYING PERSON TO PRONOUNCE THE SHAHAADAH

7.1 Mu'adh bin Jabal (May Allah be pleased with him) reported that the Messenger of Allah ﷺ said: He whose last words are: "There is no god but Allah"; (LA ILAAHA ILLALLAAH), he will enter Paradise. (Abu Dawud)

7.2 Abu Sa'id Khudri (May Allah be pleased with him) reported that the Messenger of Allah ﷺ said: Exhort the dying person to recite: "There is nothing worthy of worship but Allah". (Muslim)

CHAPTER 8

SAYING GOOD WORDS BEFORE A DYING PERSON AND HIS RELATIVES

8.1 Umm Salama (May Allah be pleased with her) reported that the Messenger of Allah ﷺ said: Whenever you visit the sick or a dying person, you should utter good words because the angels say "Amin" at what you say. She adds: When Abu Salama died, I came to the Messenger of Allah ﷺ and said: Messenger of Allah, Abu Salama has died. He directed me to supplicate: Allah, forgive me and him and bestow upon me a better future (give me a better substitute than he). So I supplicated as he had directed, and Allah gave me in exchange a man who was better for me than Abu Salama. (Muslim)

8.2 Umm Salama (Allah be pleased with her) reported that she heard the Messenger of Allah ﷺ as saying: When a person suffers from a calamity and utters: "We belong to

Allah and to Him shall we return; Allah compensate me in my affliction and give me something better in exchange for it." Umm Salama (Allah be pleased with her) said: When Abu Salama (Allah be pleased with him) died, I repeated the same sentences (of the supplication) as the Messenger of Allah ﷺ had commanded (me to do). So Allah bestowed upon me a better substitute in exchange, than him (I was married to Muhammad, the Messenger of Allah ﷺ. (Muslim)

8.3   Abu Musa al-Ash'ari (Allah be pleased with him) reported that the Messenger of Allah ﷺ said: When a man's child dies, Allah, Most High asks His angels whether they have taken out the life of the child of His servant and they reply in the affirmative. He then asks whether they have taken the fruit of his heart and they reply in the affirmative. Thereupon he asks what his servant has said. They say: He has praised You and said: We belong to Allah and to Him shall we return. Allah says: Build a house for my servant in Paradise and name it as the

House of Praise. (Tirmidhi)

8.4 Abu Huraira (Allah be pleased with him) reported that the Messenger of Allah ﷺ said: Allah, the Exalted, says: I have no reward except Paradise for a believing bondsman of Mine who displays patience when I take away his favourite one from the things of the world. (Bukhari)

8.5 Usama bin Zaid (Allah be pleased with him) narrated: A daughter of the Messenger of Allah ﷺ sent a message to him, that her son was at the last breath and requested him to come to her. The Messenger of Allah ﷺ sent back the informer saying: It is for Allah what He takes, and what He gives, and everything before His sight has a limited period. So she should expect for Allah's reward and remain patient. (Agreed upon)

CHAPTER 9

SUPPLICATION -DU'AA- TO BE RECITED SOON AFTER A PERSON DIES

9.1 Umm Salama (May Allah be pleased with her) reported that the Messenger of Allah ﷺ came to Abu Salama when his eyes were petrified (breathed his last). He closed them and said: "When the soul is taken out, the sight follows it." Some members of his family began to weep and wailed so he said: Do not supplicate for yourselves anything but good, for the angels give approval of what you utter. Then he said: "O'Allah! Forgive Abu Salama, raise his rank among those who are rightly guided and grant him successor from his descendants who remain behind. Grant us pardon and him. O' Lord of the universe! Make his grave spacious for him and give him light in it." (Muslim)

CHAPTER 10

JUSTIFICATION FOR SHEDDING TEARS AND FORBIDDANCE OF WAILING

10.1 Ibn 'Umar (Allah be pleased with him) narrated: Messenger of Allah ﷺ visited Sa'd bin 'Ubada (Allah be pleased with him) during his illness. He was accompanied by 'Abdur Rahman bin 'Auf, Sa'd bin Abi Waqqas and 'Abdullah bin Mas'ud (Allah be pleased with them). The Messenger of Allah ﷺ began to weep. When his companions saw this, they also began to shed tears. He said: Listen attentively: Allah does not punish for the shedding of tears or the grief of the heart, but takes to task or bestows mercy because of the utterances of this (and he pointed to his tongue). (Agreed upon)

10.2 Usama bin Zaid (May Allah be pleased with him) narrated: A grandson (child of the daughter) of the Messenger of Allah ﷺ was raised towards him while he was gasping (breath was irregular). The tears began to flow from the eyes of the Messenger of Allah ﷺ. Sa'd said to him: What is this, O' Allah's Messenger ﷺ? He said: It is mercy which Allah has embedded in the hearts of his slaves. Allah bestows His Mercy on the merciful among His servants. (Agreed upon)

10.3 Anas (May Allah be pleased with him) narrated: The Messenger of Allah ﷺ came to his son Ibrahim (Allah be pleased with him) when he was in the clutches of death. Allah's Messenger ﷺ started shedding tears. 'Abdur Rahman bin 'Auf (Allah be pleased with him) said, "O' Allah's Messenger ﷺ, you are also weeping. He said: O' 'Auf! It is compassion of Allah. Then he began to weep bitterly and said: The eyes are shedding tears and the heart is grieved and we will not say except what pleases our Lord. O' Ibrahim! Indeed we are grieved by your separation. (Bukhari)

CHAPTER 11

DO NOT DISCLOSE SOMETHING BAD ABOUT THE DECEASED

11.1 Abu Rufi' Aslam (may Allah be pleased with him), servant of Allah's Messenger ﷺ said: "He who washes a dead body and conceals something odious, is forgiven forty times by Allah." (Reported by Hakim)

CHAPTER 12

PARTICIPATION IN

FUNERAL PRAYERS

12.1 Abu Huraira (Allah be pleased with him) reported that the Messenger of Allah ﷺ said: Whoever follows the funeral procession and offers the funeral prayer for it, will get a reward equal to one Qirat, and whoever attends it till burial, will get a reward equal to two Qirats. It was asked, what are two Qirats? He replied; Like two huge mountains. (Agreed upon)

12.2 Abu Huraira (Allah be pleased with him) reported that the Messenger of Allah ﷺ said: Whose attends the funeral of a Muslim out of faith, seeking the reward from Allah and remains with it till the prayer is offered over it, and the burial is completed, certainly he will return with reward of two Qirats, each Qirat is equivalent to Uhud; and whose offers his prayer over it and returns before its burial, he will certainly come back with one Qirat. (Reported by Imam Al-Bukhari)

12.3 Umm 'Atiyya (Allah be pleased with her) reported that we were prohibited from accompanying a funeral procession but we were not stressed (not to do so). (Agreed upon)

CHAPTER 13

EXCELLENCE OF VAST PARTICIPATION IN FUNERAL PRAYERS AND FORMATION OF THREE ROWS OR MORE

13.1 'A'isha (Allah be pleased with her) reported that she heard the Messenger of Allah ﷺ as saying: If a company of Muslims to the number of a hundred prays over a dead person, all of them interceding for him, their intercession for him will be accepted. (Muslim)

13.2 Ibn 'Abbas (Allah be pleased with him) reported that the Messenger of Allah ﷺ said: If any Muslim dies and forty people who associate nothing with Allah, participate in the funeral prayers over him, Allah accepts them as intercessors for him. (Muslim)

13.3 Marthad bin 'Abdullah al-Yazni narrated: When Malik bin Hubaira (Allah be pleased with him) offered a funeral prayer and found a small number of participants, he divided them into three sections and remarked that Allah's Messenger ﷺ said: If three rows of men pray over anyone, his entry into paradise becomes expedient. (Abu Dawud and Tirmidhi)

CHAPTER 14

CONTENTS OF FUNERAL PRAYERS

14.1 'Abdur Rahman 'Auf bin Malik (Allah be pleased with him) reported that Allah's Messenger ﷺ offered a funeral prayer and I committed to my memory this supplication. He prayed: O' Allah! Forgive him, bestow mercy upon him, grant him salvation, pardon him, accord him a noble provision and make his grave spacious, wash him with water and snow, purify him from sins as You have purified the white garment from impurities, give him a better abode in place of his present one, and a better family in exchange of his present one and a better spouse in place of his present wife, admit him to Paradise and give him refuge from the trial in the grave and the punishment in the Hell. He narrated that the result was that he wished he should have become that dead person. (Reported by Imam Muslim)

14.2 Abu Huraira, Abu Qatada, Abu Ibrahim al-

Ashalli (Allah be pleased with them) nar-rated: Allah's Messenger ﷺ offered a funeral prayer and said: O' Allah, Forgive our living and our dead, our present and our absent, our young and our old, our male and our female. O' Allah, To whomsoever of us You give life keep him faithful to Islam while you give him life, and whomsoever of us You take in death cause his death upon faith. O' Allah, neither deprive us of his reward of faith, nor we should be subjected to trials after him. (Abu Dawud and Tirmidhi)

14.3 Abu Huraira (Allah be pleased with him) reported that he heard the Messenger of Allah ﷺ as saying: When you pray over the dead, make a sincere supplication for him. (Abu Dawud and Ibn Majah)

14.4 Abu Huraira (Allah be pleased with him) reported the Messenger of Allah ﷺ as supplicating in the course of funeral prayer over a dead body: O' Allah, You are its Lord; You created it; You guided it to Islam; You have taken its soul and You know best its inner secrets and outer aspects. We have come as intercessors, so forgive him. (Abu Dawud)

14.5 Wathila bin al-Asqa' (Allah be pleased with him) narrated: Allah's Messenger ﷺ led a funeral prayer over a Muslim in our presence. I heard him say: O' Allah, so and so son of so and so is in Your protection and inside the surroundings of Your refuge; safeguard him from the trial in the grave and the punishment in the Hell. You are Faithful and worthy to be praised. O' Allah, Pardon him and show mercy. You are the Forgiving, the Merciful one. (Abu Dawud and Ibn Majah)

14.6 'Abdullah bin Abi 'Aufa (Allah be pleased with him) narrated: While offering the funeral prayer of his daughter, he recited four takbirs and after the fourth takbir he continued standing for interval between two takbirs and besought forgiveness for her. Then he said: The Messenger of Allah ﷺ used to do so. Another version is: He recited four takbirs and remained standing in prayer for some time till I thought that he would recite the fifth takbir. Then he saluted towards the right and the left. When he turned aside we asked him about it. He replied I would add nothing to that which I saw the Messenger of Allah ﷺ do, or he said: The Messenger of Allah ﷺ used to do so. (Hakim)

CHAPTER 15

BURIAL AS SOON AS POSSIBLE AFTER DEATH

15.1 Abu Huraira (Allah be pleased with him) reported that he heard the Messenger of Allah ﷺ as saying: Hurry up with the dead body for if it was pious, you are forwarding it to welfare and if it was otherwise, you are putting off an evil thing down your necks. (Agreed upon)

15.2 Abu Sa'id al-Khudri (Allah be pleased with him) reported that the Messenger of Allah ﷺ said: When the funeral is ready, the men carry it on their shoulders. If the deceased was righteous it will say: Take it (me) away hurriedly and if he was not righteous, it will say to the members of the family; Alas! Where are you taking it (me)? Its voice is heard by everything except a human being. Had he heard it, he would have fallen into unconsciousness. (Bukhari)

CHAPTER 16

SPEEDY PAYMENT OF THE DEBTS OF THE DECEASED

16.1 Abu Huraira (Allah be pleased with him) reported that he heard the Messenger of Allah ﷺ as saying: The soul of the deceased believer remains pending on account of the debt till it is discharged. (Tirmidhi)

16.2 Husain bin Wahwah (Allah be pleased with him) narrated: Talha bin Bara' fell ill. The Messenger of Allah ﷺ came to visit him and said: Verily, I think that Talha is about to die. So you should inform me about his death and make haste (in burying him). Verily, it is improper that the corpse of a Muslim should be kept waiting by his family members. (Abu Dawud)

CHAPTER 17

ADMONITION BESIDE THE GRAVE

17.1 'Ali (Allah be pleased with him) narrated that we were accompanying a funeral procession in Baqi' Al-Gharqad (Graveyard). The Messenger of Allah ﷺ proceeded towards us and sat down. We sat ahim. He had a small stick in his hand. He was bowing down his head and scraping the ground with the stick. He said:

"There is none among you but has place assigned either in the Paradis or in the Hell.

The Companions said: O' Allah's Messenger ﷺ, should we not depend upon what has been written for us (and give up doing deeds)? The Messenger of Allah ﷺ said:

"Carry on doing good deeds. Every one will find it easy to do such deeds (as will lead him to his destined place) for which he has been created."

(Reported by Imam Al-Bukhari and Imam Muslim)

CHAPTER 18

SUPPLICATION FOR THE DECEASED AFTER HIS BURIAL

18.1 Abu 'Amr narrated on the authority of Abu 'Abdullah, Abu Laila and 'Uthman bin 'Affan (Allah be pleased with them) that the Messenger of Allah ﷺ after the burial of a dead man used to stay there and say: Seek forgiveness for your brother and supplicate for him for firmness (in faith) because he is being questioned about it. (Abu Dawud)

18.2 'Amr bin al-'As (Allah be pleased with him) is reported to have said about him; When you have buried me, you should stand near my grave till the camel is slaughtered and its meat is distributed so that I may feel you near and know what to reply to the angels, sent by my Allah. (Muslim)

CHAPTER 19

CHARITY ON BEHALF OF THE DECEASED AND PRAYING FOR HIM

19.1 Allah, the Exalted says: "And those who came after them say: Our Lord! Forgive us, and our brethren who came before us in the faith." (59:10)

19.2 'A'isha (Allah be pleased with her) narrated that a man said to the Messenger ﷺ of Allah: My mother has died suddenly. I think that if she is able to talk (while alive) she will have given alms. So, if I give alms now on her behalf, will she get the reward? The Messenger of Allah ﷺ replied in the affirmative. (Agreed upon)

19.3 Abu Huraira (Allah be pleased with him) reported that Allah's Messenger ﷺ said: When a man dies, his acts come to an end, but three; recurring charity, or knowledge by which people derive benefit, or a pious son who prays for him (for the deceased). (Muslim)

CHAPTER 20

ADMIRATION OF THE DECEASED

20.1 Anas (Allah be pleased with him) reported that some Companions happened to pass by a funeral procession (bier) and the people spoke highly of him (the deceased). The Messenger of Allah ﷺ said: It has become expedient for him. Then they passed by another funeral procession and the people spoke ill of the deceased. The Messenger of Allah ﷺ said: It has become expedient for him. 'Umar bin al-Khattab (Allah be pleased with him) submitted: Allah's Messenger ﷺ, what has become expedient? He ﷺ replied: You have praised this one, so Paradise has become expedient for him and you have spoken ill of another, so Hell has become expedient for him. You are Allah's witness on the earth. (Agreed upon)

20.2 Abu Al-Aswad (Allah be pleased with him) narrated: I came to Medina and while I was sitting beside 'Umar bin al-Khattab (Allah be pleased with him) a funeral procession passed by, the people praised the deceased. Umar bin Khattab (Allah be pleased with him) said: It is certain for him. Then another funeral procession passed by and the people spoke ill of the deceased. 'Umar bin Khattab (Allah be pleased with him) said: It is certain for him. A third funeral procession passed by and the people spoke ill of the deceased. He said: It is certain for him. I (Abu a'-Aswad) asked: O' Chief of the believers! What has become certain for him. He replied: I said the same sentences as the Messenger of Allah ﷺ had said, that is: If four persons testify the righteousness of a Muslim, Allah will grant him Paradise. We asked: If three persons testify his righteousness? He replied: Even three. Then we asked: If two? He replied: Even two. We did not ask him regarding one witness. (Bukhari)

CHAPTER 21

SUPERIORITY OF ONE WHO IS DEPRIVED OF HIS INFANTS

21.1 Anas (Allah be pleased with him) reported that the Messenger of Allah ﷺ said: A Muslim whose three children die before the age of maturity, will be granted Paradise by Allah, the Exalted due to His Mercy for them. (Agreed upon)

21.2 Abu Huraira (Allah be pleased with him) reported that the Messenger of Allah ﷺ said: A Muslim whose three children die (in infancy) will not be touched by the Fire (of the Hell) except for Allah's oath. (Agreed upon)

21.3 Abu Sa'id al-Khudri (Allah be pleased with him) reported that a woman came to the Messenger of Allah ﷺ and submitted: O' Messenger of Allah! Men derive benefit out of your utterances. Please fix a day for us, so that you may impart us the religious knowledge which Allah has taught you. The Messenger of Allah ﷺ appointed one day and directed them to assemble. When they gathered, the Messenger of Allah ﷺ went to them and said: A woman whose three children die will be screened from the Fire (of Hell) by virtue of them. One of the woman asked: If two has died? The Messenger of Allah ﷺ replied: Even two will screen her from the Fire (of the Hell). (Agreed upon)

CHAPTER 22

WEEPING OVER THE REMAINS
OF THE EVIL DOERS

22.1 Ibn 'Umar (Allah be pleased with him) narrated: When the Messenger of Allah ﷺ and his Companions were passing near Hijr, the habitations of the Thamud, he admonished his Companions: Do not pass by these tormented ones, except with eyes shedding tears. Do not pass near them without weeping lest the calamity should fall upon you as it had fallen to their lot. (Agreed upon)

Another version is: When the Messenger of Allah ﷺ passed near Hijr, he said: Do not enter but weepingly the habitations of the persons who committed tyranny lest the same chastisement should fall upon you as it fell upon them. The Messenger of Allah ﷺ covered his head and urged his mount to proceed quickly and passed through the valley of the tormented people hurriedly.

PART-II

JANAAZAH AND RELATED MATTERS

CHAPTER 23

INTRODUCTION TO THE JANAAZAH

Nothing in this world is permanent. Ultimately the entire phenomenal world will pass away. The magnificent creation of Allah, the heavenly bodies and the earth with its living creatures; the splendours of human glory, the wonders of science and art, will come to an end ultimately.

The Holy Quran says:

﴾ لاَ إِلٰهَ إِلاَّ هُوَ كُلُّ شَيءٍ هَالِكٌ إِلَّا وَجْهُهُ ﴿

"There is no Allah but He. Everything (that exists) is gradually being disintegrated, except His Own Self. "(28:88)

Sooner or later, every soul shall have a taste of death.

﴾ كُلُّ نَفْسٍ ذَائِقَةُ الْمَوْتِ ﴿

"Every soul shall have a taste of death." (3:185)

No matter where we may be death will come to snatch us away from this temporary world of ours.

﴿ أَيْنَمَا تَكُونُوا يُدْرِككُّمُ الْمَوْتُ وَلَوْ كُنْتُمْ فِي بُرُوجٍ مُّشَيَّدَةٍ ﴾

"*Wherever you are, death will find you out, even if you are in tower built up strong and high.*" (4:78)

Abdullah bin Umar told of the Messenger of Allah ﷺ, taking him by the shoulders and saying:

"*Be in the world as though you are a stranger or one who is passing through.*"

DEATH - THE GATEWAY TO A HIGHER LIFE

Death is but the gateway to a higher life and an essential stage in the process of the human life cycle. The human frame is a vehicle for the soul to develop itself. When the soul departs from the body, it leaves the body for good and adopts another kind of body. The soul has to evolve itself from the crude form of simple conscious-ness to a certain stage of spirituality. For the soul to unfold its infinite potentialities of advancement, it has been Divinely ordained for every soul to have a taste of death.

After departing from the physical body, the soul will not enter its life of or hell at once. When entering the grave the soul will remain suspended in the condition called BARZAKH which literally means "partition." Here its faculties will remain in abeyance, though intact, and this state will continue till the Day of Judgement when it will be sent to either heaven or hell. The impressions which it has acquired on earth through its actions will come to the surface. Character being the crystallization of one's thoughts, "the thoughts that he or she was thinking in this world take their shape; virtuous thoughts take happy shapes, and wicked thoughts take shapes of calamities according to what he believed in this world."

HELL (JAHANNAM)

The souls which are suffering from spiritual diseases and do not comply with the required standard will be sent to Hell or Jahannam. Hell will be one stage in the process of evolution for the soul that has not utilized the opportunities provided to it in its earthly sojourn and has stunted its faculties and got diseased and corrupted. After suffering the consequences of its evil actions on earth, it shall come out of that state and shall continue on its journey. Imaam Bukhari records a tradition of the Holy Prophet ﷺ to this effect:

> "*When the sinners shall have attained TAQDHIB and TANQIYAH, they will be allowed to enter heaven.*"

TAQDHIB literally means the cutting of the branches of a tree so that the tree may enjoin a more luxurious growth; and TANQIYAH means the separating of the corrupt and corruptible parts from a thing in order to purify it completely.

HEAVEN (JANNAH)

The souls which attained the required standard of perfection will start on their journey anew in the next world. The impressions of their actions on earth will, because of the rightness of their actions, unclothe the soul in a garb of undefinable happiness and light (NOOR).

According to a HADITH, Allah has provided for the righteous that which "no eye hath seen, no ear has heard, nor has it ever occurred to the mind of man." The climax of the blessings of heaven will be reached in the vision of Allah and in living in His Holy Presence.

The Quran says:

﴿ إِنَّ الْمُتَّقِيْنَ فِي جَنَّاتٍ وَّنَهَرٍ ٥ فِي مَقْعَدِ صِدْقٍ عِنْدَ مَلِيْكٍ مُّقْتَدِرٍ ﴾

"As to the righteous they will be in the midst of Gardens and Rivers, in an Assembly of Truth, in the presence of a Sovereign Omnipotent." *(54:54-55)*

﴿ وَجُوهُ يَوْمِئِذٍ نَاضِرَةٌ ٥ إِلَى رَبِّهَا نَاظِرَةٌ ﴾

"Some faces, that Day, will beam (in brightness and beauty); - looking towards their Lord." (75:22-23)

﴿ تَحِيَّتُهُمْ يَوْمَ يَلْقَوْنَهُ سَلَامٌ وَأَعَدَّ لَهُمْ أَجْراً كَرِيماً ﴾

"Their salutation on the Day they meet Him will be "Peace!"; and He has prepared for them a generous reward." (33:44)

Heavenly life is a life which consists in the unfolding of the latent faculties of the soul and its complete growth. It is a life of fruition and unlimited progress. The Quran uses the term FALAAH for this fruition. FALAAH literally means the furrowing out of the latent faculties, and as the ordinary peasant or FALAAH needs rain for his crop, so too man needs a rain. That rain comes from Allah in the form of revelation. Thus if man wants to reap a good harvest he must become a receptacle for this rain.

CHAPTER 24

WHAT TO DO WHEN A PERSON IS ON THE VERGE OF DYING

When a person, male or female, is very ill and on the verge of dying, the following acts are SUNNAH:

1. To have his face turned towards the QIBLAH and to make him lie on his right side. If it is difficult, he should be left lying flat on his back, with legs towards the QIBLAH, and the head raised. In this way, his head should be facing the QIBLAH.

2. For a person dear to him to sit on his right and repeat the KALIMAH continuously. Other relatives and friends present around the dying person should also recite the KALIMAH: "LAA ILAAHA ILLALLAAH" "There is none worthy to be worshipped except Allah."

The Messenger of Allah (ﷺ) said:

Advise the dying person to say, LA ILAAHA ILLALLAAH (There is nothing worthy of worship except Allah), because a dying Muslim who recites this will be saved from Hell.

The idea of repeating the KALIMAH continuously is to help him to fix his trust in Allah and to enable him to breathe his last with the KALIMAH on his lips. This recital of the KALIMAH before death is referred to as the TALQEEN, the prayer of suggestion. There is another TALQEEN which is recited at the grave after the burial.

3. The relatives and friends present should pray that mercy, forgiveness and blessings of Allah be given to the deceased.

4. To recite beside him SURAH YAASEEN, i.e., CHAPTER 36 of the Holy Qur'an.

Ma'qil reported that the Messenger of Allah said ﷺ:
"Recite SURAH YAASEEN before the dying among you."

The Messenger ﷺ of Allah also said:
"Recitation of Surah Yaseen eases the pain of dying; the grave becomes

spacious; and on the Day of Resurrec-
tion, the person will rise looking
fresh." [ABU DAWOOD]

It is also SUNNAH to recite SURAH RA'D, i.e., SURAH 13, before the dying person.

The recitals should not be in a loud voice lest it annoys the dying person. After his death and before he has been washed, it is MAKROOH to recite any verse of the Quran near him.

5.   To apply perfume to him and to have a pleasant fragrance in the room.

6.   It is advised that people present should talk about the mercy, blessings and forgiveness of Allah. The dying person should have a very pleasant feeling towards Allah, hoping for the best to come from Him. The Holy prophet Muhammad (ﷺ) said: "At the time of death a person should expect the best from Allah and hope that he will have mercy on him and will forgive him."

7.   The dying person should be able to over-come the fear of death. This can be done

when he sees a good number of relatives and friends around him. For at that time the dying person enters into a period of strange feelings and acute understanding.

8. The dying person may wish to talk to someone about his experience. Presence of a religious leader may help in a peaceful death. He would feel less lonely, but more dignified.

9. The presence of loved ones, friends and religious leader may help the dying person to ask forgiveness from them and request them to pray for him. Thus, he would feel less troubled and more happy than before.

10. Relatives should encourage the dying person to make bequests and SADAQAH JAAR-IYAH.

11. It is advisable to treat the departing person as a forerunner who is going ahead of us, for we will join him very soon.

WHAT A SICK PERSON SHOULD DO

A person who is sick should observe patience, make DHIKR as much as possible, and especially recite the KALIMAH.

CHAPTER 25

THE IMPORTANCE OF MAKING
A WILL (WASIYYAH)

It is of the greatest importance for every Muslim who owns property to make a will (WASIYYAH) according to the requirements of the SHARI'AH. The urgent importance for every Muslim owning property to make a will cannot be over-stressed. Failure to fulfil this obligation has often been the cause of unnecessary legal expenses, much bitterness and strife, leading sometimes to permanent estrangement between members of the family. All this can so easily be avoided by simply drawing up a will.

Allah expressly sanctions the making of a will in the Holy Quran:

﴿ كُتِبَ عَلَيْكُمْ إِذَا حَضَرَ أَحَدَكُمُ الْمَوْتُ إِنْ تَرَكَ خَيْرًا الْوَصِيَّةُ لِلْوَالِدَيْنِ وَالْأَقْرَبِينَ بِالْمَعْرُوفِ حَقًّا عَلَى الْمُتَّقِينَ ﴾

"It is prescribed, when death approaches

any of you, if he leave any goods, that he make a bequest to parents and next of kin, according to reasonable usage; this is due from the God-fearing." (2:180)

It is also an important requirement when a will is made, that it be properly witnessed. Almighty Allah states in the Holy Qur'an :

﴿ يَا أَيُّهَا الَّذِينَ آمَنُوا شَهَادَةُ بَيْنِكُم إِذَا حَضَرَ أَحَدَكُمُ الْمَوْتُ حِينَ الْوَصِيَّةِ اثْنَانِ ذَوَا عَدْلٍ مِّنْكُم ... ﴾

YAA AYYUHAL- LA-DHIINA AA-MANUU SHA-HAADATU BAYNI-KUM I-DHAA HADARA AHADAKUM-MUL- MAWTU HI-INAL- WASIY-YA-TITH- NAANI DHAWAA 'ADLIN MINKUM

O you who believe! When death approaches any of you, (take) witnesses among yourselves when making bequests - two just men of your own (brotherhood) (5:109)

The power of the testator to dispose of his property as he personally decides in accordance with the requirements of equity, extends over only one-third of the property; the remaining two-thirds are distributed among heirs as specified by the SHARI'AH. The restriction of legacies to one-third rests upon the HADITH that the Prophet ﷺ forbade Sa'd Ibn Abi Waqqas [R.A.] for bequeathing more than one-third of his estate. On the authority of Sa'd Ibn Abi Waqqas [R.A.] who said: "The Messenger of Allah, ﷺ used to visit me at Makkah, in the year of the Farewell pilgrimage, on account of (my) illness which had become very severe. I said, 'My illness has become very severe and I have much property and there is none to inherit from me but a daughter. Shall I then bequeath two-thirds of my property as a charity?' He said, "No." I said, "Half?" He said, "No." Then he said:

"Bequeath one-third and one-third is much, for if you leave your heirs free from want, it is better than you leave them in want, begging of (other) people; and you don't spend anything seeking thereby the pleasure of Allah but you are rewarded for it, even for that which you put into the mouth of your wife."

Since the Holy Qur'an has fixed the shares of the heirs as stated in SURAH 4, verses 11-12, and in the light of the above HADITH, the heirs may not be deprived altogether. A legacy in favour of one heir is invalid, unless the other heirs approve of it, but their consent is immaterial if it is given in the lifetime of the testator. All distribution takes place after the legacies and debts (including funeral expenses) have first been paid.

CHAPTER 26

DU'AA FOR A SICK PERSON

When visiting a sick person, it is SUNNAH to recite the following DU'AA:

Bismilla-hish shaa-fee* bismilla-hilkaafee-'*bis-milla-hilmu-'aafee* bismillaa-hil ladhee laa yadur-ruma-'as-mihee shai-un fil ardi walaa fis samaa-i wa hu-was samee-'ul ' aleem* as-a-lullahal azeema rabbal 'arshil kareem an yash-feeka shi-faa-an kaa-milan* adh-hibil ba'- sa rabban naas* wash-fi antash shaa-fee laa shifaa-a illaa shifaa-uka shifaa-an laa yu-ghaa-diru sa-qamaa.

In the name of Allah, the Healer; in the name of Allah, the Self-Sufficient; in the name of Allah, the One Who is free of any physical deficiency; in the name of Allah, with Whose name nothing, either on the earth or in the sky, can do any harm. He is the One Who hears and knows everything. I beg of Allah, the Magnificent, the Lord of the Magnificent Throne, to cure thee, a perfect cure. Remove this harm, O Lord of mankind, and cure! Thou art the Healer. There is no cure save Thine. Bring about a cure that will leave no sickness.

CHAPTER 27

WHAT TO DO WHEN DEATH HAS COME TO A PERSON

When death has come to a person, male or female, it is SUNNAH to carry out the following acts:

*   To close his eyes while saying:

    Bismilla-hi wa 'alaa millati rasoo-lillaa.

    In the name of Allah, and in accordance with the religion of the Messenger of Allah.

*   Thereafter recite the following DU'AA:

Allah-hummagh firlahu (lahaa)* war-fa' dara-jatahu (haa) fil mah-diyyeen* wakhlufhu fee aqi-bihee (haa) fil faa-izeen* waghfir lanaa wa lahu (lahaa) yaa rabbal 'aalameen* wafsah lahu (lahaa) fee qabri-hee (haa)* wa nawwir lahu (lahaa) feeh.

O Allah! Forgive him (her) and raise his (her) position among the rightly-guided. Let someone from among his (her) survivors fill his (her) place after him (her): Forgive us and him (her), O Lord of the worlds! And make his (her) grave spacious for him (her); and illuminate it for him (her).

* To tie a band of cloth around the head and chin.

* To loosen the joints and gently fold them.

* To straighten his head.

* To clean up all secretions.

* To place the MAYYIT (the deceased) on an elevated place like a bed or an ablution bier.

* To keep his face and the soles of his feet directed towards the QIBLAH.

* To cover the entire body, including his head, with a soft sheet.

* To place one end of the sheet under his head

and the bottom end under his feet.

* To hasten with the preparation for the burial once it has been established without any doubt that the person has died.

* To inform relatives and friends so that they may attend the JANAAZAH.

* To repeat the following words when news of death is received.

« إِنَّا لِلَّهِ وَإِنَّا إِلَيْهِ رَاجِعُونَ »

INNAA LILLAAHI WA INNAA ILAYHI RAAJI'UUN.

"To Allah we belong, and to Him is our return."

* To refrain from abusing the dead.

Aishah reported that the prophet ﷺ said:

"Do not abuse the dead, for they have gone on to what they sent before."

* To obtain a doctor's certificate.

* To obtain a death certificate.

*   To obtain the requirements for the washing (GHUSL), shrouding (KAFAN) and burial (DAFN).

*   To obtain a burial order for the preparation of a grave (QABR).

*   To arrange transport if the cemetery (MAQ-BARAH) is very far.

*** To make other necessary arrangements. You can contact the nearest Masjid / Islamic Centre for any assistance you may need.

CHAPTER 28

CHARITY ON BEHALF OF THE DEAD

Charity on behalf of the dead is a source of benefit to them. In the early days of Islam charity on behalf of the dead was generally practiced.

Aishah reported that a man said to the Prophet ﷺ : My mother died a sudden death, and I am sure that if she had been able to speak she would have given in charity; will she have a reward if I give in charity on her behalf? He (the Holy Prophet ﷺ) said "Yes."

It is reported on the authority of Sa'd ibn Ubaadah that:

His mother died while he was absent. So he said, O Messenger of Allah ﷺ ! My mother died while I was absent; will it benefit her if I give in charity on her behalf? He (the Holy Prophet ﷺ) said, "Yes." He said, "Then I make thee a witness that my orchard MIKHRAAF is a charity on her behalf."

Instead of the bereaved family preparing food to feed those who had participated in the observance of the funeral rites - a practice for which there is no basis in the Shari'ah, and which cannot be considered as an act of charity since in most cases it is not for the benefit of the poor - the commendable practice according to the SUNNAH is for some near relative, friend or neighbour of the deceased to send food to the bereaved family. There is also no authentic hadith of the Holy Prophet ﷺ for the ceremonies connected with the third, seventh, fortieth and hundredth day after death. Providing food or cake on the occasions of these ceremonies to people who are not from among the poor cannot be considered an act of charity. The proper course to adopt with the object of giving charity on behalf of the dead would be to feed and help the distressed and oppressed and to make an endowment for the spiritual, moral and educational development of society.

CHAPTER 29

OUR OBLIGATIONS TO THE DEAD

When a Muslim dies, there are four obligations that the community owe to him. These four obligations are:

a) BATHING THE CORPSE **GHUSL**

b) ENSHROUDING THE **CORPSE KAFAN**

c) OFFERING PRAYER FOR THE REPOSE OF THE DEAD **SALAAT-UL-JANAAZAH**

d) BURYING THE CORPSE **DAFAN**

Each of these four acts, according to the SHARI'AH is classified as a FARDU KI-FAAYAH, i.e., an act which every Muslim is under obligation to perform, until a sufficient number of persons have performed it, the rest being then absolved from the obligation of performance. The reward (AJR) in such case, belongs to those who performed the act, but the rest are not punished for their omission. If, however, no one should perform the act, then they are all liable to punishment.

CHAPTER 30

BATHING THE CORPSE - GHUSL

The obligation of GHUSL can be fulfilled by a total washing of the corpse once only provided the water reaches every part of the skin. The washing of the body three, five or seven times is SUNNAH.

THE CONDITIONS (SHUROOT) OF GHUSL

For a valid performance of GHUSL of the MAYYIT, the following conditions should be observed:

* The MAYYIT should be a Muslim. It is, however, permissible to wash the corpse of a non-Muslim.

* There must be at least a part of body of the deceased available for GHUSL.

* The deceased must not be a SHAHEED (martyr) who had died in a war fought in the

cause of Allah. As regards the Muslims who were slain in the battle of Uhud the Prophet (ﷺ) said:

"Do not wash them. Verily from every wound or blood an aroma of musk will emanate on the Day of Judgement, and dnot perform SAL-AAH over them."

According to Imaam Shafi'i, neither GHUSL nor SALAAT-UL-JANAAZAH are necessary for the SHAHEED in the battle field. It is also of no consequence whether the SHAHEED is in a state of HADATH AKBAR or HADATH ASGHAR. Imaam Abu Hanifah, however, holds that the Funeral Prayer is necessary, but not GHUSL.

WHEN A CORPSE HAS BEEN RECOV-ERED FROM A BODY OF WATER

Even when a corpse has been recovered from a body of water, the FARD act of bathing it can be fulfilled only by pouring water over the entire body once or thrice.

THE CASE OF A MISCARRIAGE

*   In the case of a miscarriage after a pregnancy period of six months, GHUSL and SALAAH should be performed.

*   Where the miscarriage occurs before six months and it is established that there was life, GHUSL and SALAAH are necessary.

*   If there is no sign of human form, then neither GHUSL nor SALAAH is necessary.

*   In the case of a miscarriage on whom GHUSL and SALAAH are necessary, it is SUNNAH to name the child.

TAYAMMUM - A SUBSTITUTE FOR GHUSL

TAYAMMUM can act as a substitute for GHUSL in the following circumstances:

*   When water is not available.

*   When the use of water on a person who, for instance, had been burnt to death, may

result in the disintegration of the body.

If the pouring of water over a burnt body does not cause the body to disintegrate, then TAYAMMUM is not allowed. In such a case the water should only be poured over the body without any rubbing or washing.

WHO SHOULD PERFORM THE GHUSL

*   It is HARAAM for males to bathe females or for females to bathe males with the exception of married couples who may perform GHUSL on each other.

*   An adult male should be bathed by his father, son or brother. An adult female by her mother, daughter or sister. In the absence of these persons, any near relative may carry out this duty. In the absence of a relative any capable and righteous Muslim may be requested to execute this rite with the assistance of others.

*   If a male passes away - on a journey, for instance - and there are no males to bathe

him, then besides his wife, only a person whom he cannot marry (a MAHRAM) such as his mother, daughter or sister is permitted to perform the GHUSL, otherwise TAYAM-MUM by a Muslim stranger should be performed. The same rule applies to a female who passes away and there are no females to bathe her. In the absence of her husband or any MAHRAM, TAYAMMUM should be performed on her.

If the MAYYIT is a girl who has not yet attained the age of puberty, then it is permissible for an unrelated male to wash her. The same rule applies if the MAYYIT is a boy who has not yet attained the age of puberty: it is permissible for an unrelated female to wash him. The GHAASIL should be a trustworthy person. Should he see anything objectionable on the MAYYIT, he should not disclose it to others.

ACTS THAT ARE MAKROOH TO CARRY OUT ON THE MAYYIT

It is MAKROOH to carry out the following acts on the MAYYIT:

* To cut the MAYYIT'S nails,

* the hair on the head,

* the hair under the armpits,

* the pubic hairs, and

* the moustache and the beard.

THE METHOD OF PERFORMING GHUSL

1. Ensure that the GHUSL of the MAYYIT is performed in a secluded place with only the GHAASIL (the one who washes) and his assistants in attendance.

2. Place the MAYYIT on an ablution bier or a raised platform with the soles of the feet turned towards the QIBLAH and the head raised higher than the feet so that the used water may not flow back onto the corpse.

3. Fumigate the area around the ablution bier with frankincense so as to neutralised any odour the body may give off.

4. Cover the MAYYIT with a sheet particularly the AWRAH which for males is that part of the body from the navel to below the knees and for females from above the breast to the ankles.

5. According to the SHAFI'I MADH-HAB it is preferable to use cold water since it delays decomposition. Only in cases of extreme cold or where the MAYYIT is very dirty should warm water be used. According to the HANAFI MADH-HAB the use of warm water is preferable.

6. Raise the MAYYIT gently to a sitting position. Place the right hand on the shoulder blade and the thumb on the nape of the neck and with the right knee support the back of the MAYYAT.

7. Press down hard upon the stomach with the left hand and repeat this action, called ISTIBRAA, in order to discharge any excreta which may be inside the MAYYIT.

8. Pour water freely and continuously while ISTIBRAA is applied.

9.   Lower the MAYYIT gently on its back after completing the ISTIBRAA.

10. Wrap a piece of cloth round the left hand and thoroughly wash the private parts without looking at them or touching them with the bare hands.

11. After washing the private parts discard the cloth and wash the hands thoroughly with soap.

12. Wrap another piece of cloth round the right fingers, moisten them and clean the teeth and nostrils.

13. Give WUDOO to the MAYYIT. The GHAA-SIL should resolve in his mind to perform WUDOO and may formulate the NIYYAH as follows: "I hereby intend to perform WUDOO on this MAYYIT." Perform WUDOO in the usual manner. 14. After the WUDOO, wash the head, face, neck and ears with soap or any other cleansing agent. If these are not available, pure water will suffice. If there are any plaits, they should be loosened and combed with a comb whose teeth are wide

apart. Any hair that may come out should be placed with the MAYYIT in the KAFAN.

15. Wash the front part of the body with soap, from the neck downwards to the feet, first the right side and then the left.

16. Rinse the body by pouring water from the head down to the feet.

17. Tilt the body onto its left side and wash its back with soap from the neck downwards to the feet.

18. Tilt the body onto its right side and wash its back in the same manner.

19. Rinse the body by pouring water from the head down to the feet.

20. Pour pure water in which camphor has been dissolved over the whole body. This last GHUSL is the one which is regarded as the FARDU KIFAAYAH. This is also the stage when the NIYYAH for GHUSL should be made.

If the body is still dirty after three such washings,

then it should be washed once more. It is SUNNAH to perform the washings an odd-number of times - three, five or seven times.

21. The body should then be dried with a clean towel.

CHAPTER 31

SHROUDING THE CORPSE - KAFAN

THE SECOND SOCIAL OBLIGATION

The second obligation we owe to the dead is to wrap the body of the MAYYIT in shrouds or KAFAN after the GHUSL has been completed. The KAFAN are thus the grave clothes of the deceased.

THE KAFAN REQUIREMENTS

*   The MASNOON (prescribed as SUNNAH) KAFAN consists of three shrouds for the male and female, each shroud covering the body of the MAYYIT.

*   It is, however, permissible to add an extra two wrappings, viz., a shirt (QAMEES) and a turban or veil (KHIMAAR) to the three. For a female the five pieces are the completest form of KAFAN. If only three shrouds are used, the body is simply enshrouded three times.

84

*   The minimum KAFAN is one wrapping but is MAKROOH to use less than two without a valid reason.

*   As regards the material for KAFAN the Prophet ﷺ said: "Do not be extravagant in shrouding, for it will decay quickly."

*   It is commendable to use white calico which has been washed.

*   It is HARAAM to use silk as KAFAN for a man if other cloth is available. It will, however, be permissible (JAA-IZ) but MAK-ROOH to enshroud a woman, child or an insane person with silk or coloured cloth.

    Ibn Abbas reported that the Messenger of Allah said: "Wear your white garments, for they are among your best garments, and shroud your dead in them....."

*   If the only KAFAN available is dirty and cannot be cleaned, the SALAAH should be performed on the MAYYIT and afterwards wrapped in the available KAFAN.

* When cloth is not available, skins or weeds or clusters of leaves, in order of preference, may be used.

* Other KAFAN requirements are cotton wool and aromatic spices such as sweet-smelling oil like bergamot oil and frankincense in powdered form and some camphor.

* It is HARAAM to write in ink any passage from the Quraor any of the Excellent Names (ASMAA-UL-HUSNAA) of Allah either on the body or shroud of the MAYYIT.

WHO SHOULD PROVIDE THE KAFAN

* The KAFAN should be bought with the earnings of the deceased him/herself.

* If the deceased left no money behind, it is the reponsibility of those who supported him/her financially to provide the KAFAN.

* Where a family lack the means to provide the KAFAN, the BAIT-UL-MAL (the treasury of the community) should do so, otherwise the general public should provide the KAFAN.

THE METHOD OF ENSHROUDING THE MAYYIT

1. Spread out the first shroud on the floor, on it the second and finally the third on the second.

2. If available, apply grated camphor, incense, rose leaves and perfume on each shroud.

3. Lower the body gently onto the KAFAN so that the MAYYIT lies on its back.

4. Place the right hand over the left on the chest or place them on the sides.

5. Place camphorated pads of cotton wool on the SUJOOD parts, namely, the forehead, nose, hands, knees and feet, as well as under the buttocks so that the posterior ring is covered. It is also SUNNAH to pad the genitals, anus and wounds, if any, with cotton wool.

If there are any discharges from the mouth or nose then these should be covered with cotton wool to protect the KAFAN from becoming soiled.

6.   Press the thighs together.

7.   Fold the left flap of the top shroud tightly over the body and the right flap tightly over the left.

The other two wrappings are folded in the same manner.

8.   Fasten the ends of the shrouds at the head and feet and around the middle with strips of cloth.

The shrouding of the male and female is carried out in the same manner, except that the female is first shrouded with a covering below the waist (IZAAR), a cloak (QAMEES) which comes over the head and arms covering the entire body and a veil after which it is shrouded with the two shrouds.

In the case of a person dying while in the state of IHRAAM no perfume should be applied to his/her body or KAFAN. The male pilgrim's head should not be wrapped in KAFAN nor the face of the female pilgrim.

CHAPTER 32

THE FUNERAL PRAYER - SALAATUL JANAAZAH

THE THIRD SOCIAL OBLIGATION

A prayer-service over the dead body (MAYYIT) of every Muslim, young or old, even of infants who have lived a few minutes or seconds, is performed. This is the third social obligation (FARDU KIFAAYAH) that we owe to the dead.

The prayer may be held in a mosque, or in an open space or even in the graveyard if sufficient space be available there. According to the HANAFI and MALIKI MADH-HAB it is MAK-ROOH to perform SALAATUL JANAAZAH in a mosque or to bring the MAYYIT into the mosque.

THE ESSENTIALS (ARKAAN) OF THE FUNERAL PRAYER

The Funeral Prayer or SALAAT-UL-JANAAZAH is governed by seven ARKAAN or essential acts. The omission or incorrect performance of any of these ARKAAN will render the SALAAH null and void (BAATIL).

1. Occupying the mind with the intention (NIYYAH) at the commencement of SALAAH.

2. Assuming the standing position (QIYAAM) from the beginning to the end of SALAAH, if one is able to do so.

3. Pronouncing FOUR TAKBIRS, including the TAKBIRAT-UL-IHRAAM.

At the pronouncement of each TAKBIR the hands are raised to the ears and folded below the chest in the usual manner.

4. Reciting the FATIHAH after the first TAK-BIR. Even when the JANAAZAH Prayer is offered at night time, it is SUNNAH to recite the FATIHAH and DU'AAS silently. Only the Imaam should pronounce the TAKBIRS and TASLIM loudly.

5. Reciting the SALAWAAT after the second TAKBIR.

6. Reciting one of the well-known DU'AAS for the deceased after the third TAKBIR.

7. Pronouncing the TASLIM after the fourth TAKBIR.

THE CONDITIONS (SHUROOT) OF
THE JANAAZAH PRAYER

1. The deceased should be a Muslim. It is HARAAM to perform the JANAAZAH Prayer over a non-Muslim deceased, on the basis of the Quranic injunction:

﴿ وَلَا تُصَلِّ عَلَى أَحَدٍ مِّنْهُمْ مَّاتَ أَبَدًا وَلَا تَقُمْ عَلَى قَبْرِهِ إِنَّهُمْ كَفَرُوا بِاللَّهِ وَرَسُولِهِ وَمَاتُوا وَهُمْ فَاسِقُونَ ﴾

Do not pray for any of them that dies, nor stand at his grave, for they rejected Allah and His Messenger and they died in a state of perverse rebellion. (9:84)

It is, however, necessary to wrap the non-Muslim's body with cloth, and to bury the body in a grave. This obligation will, of course, be fulfilled even when non-Muslims perform it.

2. The corpse should have been bathed or TAYAMMUM should have been given to it.

As pointed out above, in the case of the SHAHEED or martyr who should not be bathed, no SALAAH is offered over him, nor should his body be enshrouded. It will be best to use his blood-stained garments as his KAFAN. It is not necessary to remove the blood clots on his body.

3. The corpse should be in front of those offering the Prayer. It is SUNNAH for the Imaam to stand opposite the head of the male deceased and opposite the waist of the female deceased. The followers should stand behind the Imaam preferably in three or more rows.

THE SHUROOT OF THE JANAAZAH PRAYER PERTAINING TO THE ONE WHO PRAYS (MUSALLEE)

These are similar to the conditions that apply to the one who performs SALAAH on other occasions:

* One should be pure from HADATH.

* One should be pure from NAJJIS.

* One should face the QIBLAH.

* One's AWRAH should be covered.

* One should observe all the necessary rules pertaining to the JANAAZAH Prayer.

TIMES WHEN THE JANAAZAH PRAYER SHOULD NOT BE PERFORMED

It is MAKROOH to perform the JANAAZAH Prayer at the following times:-

* When the sun rises.

* When the sun passes the meridian (ZA-WAAL).

* When the sun sets.

Besides these three times which last for a very short period, the JANAAZAH Prayer could be performed at any time during the day or night. It could also be offered after the ASR Prayer.

THE SUNNAHS OF THE JANAAZAH

They are:

*   Expressing the NIYYAH.

*   Reciting the TA'AWWUDH at the beginning of the FATIHAH.

*   Reciting the TA'MEEN at the end of the FATIHAH.

*   Reciting the TAKBIRS, the FAATIHAH and the DU'AAS silently. Only the Imam should recite the TAKBIRS and SALAAM aloud.

*   Performing the Salaah in congregation.

*   Standing behind the Imaam, preferably in three rows or an odd number of rows (SUFOOF).

*   Reciting the completest form of the SALA-WAAT on the Prophet as given under "THE METHOD OF PERFORMING THE JANAZ-

ZAH PRAYER."

* Reciting the SALAWAAT on the Prophet's family and Companions.

* Praying for the believing men and women after the SALAWAAT.

* The Imaam should stand opposite the head of the male deceased and opposite the waist of the female deceased.

* Raising the hands to the ears at the every TAKBIR and folding them below the chest.

WHO SHOULD LEAD THE JANAAZAH PRAYER

The person most deserving of leading the JANAAZAH Prayer, in order of precedence, is as follows:-

1. The father, grandfather or great-grandfather, in order of ascendancy.

2. The most righteous son, grandson, etc., in

order of ascendancy.

3.   The blood-brother, the step-brother, the blood-brother's son and then the step-brother's son in the aforementioned order.

4.   The paternal relatives of the father, grand-father or great- grandfather.

5.   The appointed Imaam of the community or his deputy.

6.   The maternal male relatives of the de-ceased, the nearest relative to the de-ceased taking precedence.

7.   The one whose knowledge of FIQH (Islamic Jurisprudence) is best.

8.   After him, the one who knows the Quran best.

9.   Finally the one who is the most upright should lead.

*   In the case of the deceased having directed in his WASIYYAH or will that someone should lead the JANAAZAH Prayer over him, but who,

according to the SHARI'AH has no right to lead, then the WASIYYAH should be waived.

*   When a person who has the greatest right in regard to the deceased is absent at the time of the funeral, the JANAAZAH Prayer may be delayed till such time as he arrives, if it is known that he will arrive before the body starts decomposing.

THE METHOD OF PERFORMING
THE JANAAZAH PRAYER

1.   Place the MAYYIT in front with the head on the right side of the Imaam.

2.   The Imaam or MUNFARID (the one who prays alone) should stand opposite the head of the deceased if the deceased is a male and opposite the waist if the deceased is a female.

3.   Form an odd number of ranks(SAFF) close to one another because no SUJOODS have to be performed.

4. Let someone chant the IQAAMAH for the JANAAZAH Prayer. If the deceased is a female the call is as follows:

*ASSA-LAATU 'ALAL MAIYI-TA-TIL HAA-DIRAH * ASSA-LAATU RAHI-MAKUMULLAH.* Come to SALAAH for the deceased female that is present here! The SALAAH is a mercy of Allah upon you!

If the deceased is a male the IQAAMAH is slightly different:

*ASSA-LAATU 'ALAL MAIYI-TIL HAADIR * ASSA-LAATU RAHI-MAKUMULLAH.* Come to SALAAH for the deceased male that is present here! The SALAAH is a mercy of Allah upon you!

5. The NIYYAH to perform the JANAAZAH Prayer should now be resolved and expressed as follows:

Nawaitu usalle ar-ba-'a takbee-raatin alaa man hadara min amwaa-til muslimeena farda ki-faa-yah (ma'-muuman) lil-laahi ta-'aalaa.

I hereby resolve to pray four TAKBIRS as a FARD KIFAAYAH upon (the deceased) who is present here from among the deceased Muslims, as a follower of the Imaam, for the sake of Allah, the Most High.

6. Immediately after the NIYYAH, the hands are raised to the ears while the FIRST TAKBIR (TAKBIRAT-UL-IHRAAM) is pronounced:

Allahu Akbar!
Allah is Greatest!

The hands are then folded below the chest in the usual manner.

7. The TA'AWWUDH is then recited:

A-'oodhu billaa-hi mi-nash shaytaa-nir rajeem. I seek refuge with Allah from Satan, the accursed devil.

8. This is followed by the FAATIHAH:

﴿ اَلْحَمْدُ لِلَّهِ رَبِّ الْعَالَمِيْنَ ○ الرَّحْمٰنِ الرَّحِيْمِ ○ مَالِكِ يَوْمِ الدِّيْنِ ○ إِيَّاكَ نَعْبُدُ وَإِيَّاكَ نَسْتَعِيْنُ ○ إِهْدِنَا الصِّرَاطَ الْمُسْتَقِيْمَ صِرَاطَ الَّذِيْنَ أَنْعَمْتَ عَلَيْهِمْ غَيْرِ الْمَغْضُوْبِ عَلَيْهِمْ وَلَا الضَّالِّيْنَ ﴾ آمِيْن .

Bismillaa-hir rah-maa-nir raheem*
Al-hamdu lillaa-hi rabbil 'aalameen
* ar-rahmaa-nir ra-heem * maaliki
yaw-mid-deen * iyyaaka na'budu wa
iyyaaka nas-ta-een * ihdi-nas siraa-
talmus-taqeem * siraa-tal-ladheena
an-'amta 'alaihim ghairil maghdoobi
alaihim * walad-daal-leen *

In the name of Allah, Most Gracious, Most Merciful. Praise be to Allah, the Cherisher and Sustainer of the Worlds; Most Gracious, Most Merciful; Master of the Day of Judgement. Thee do we worship, and Thine aid we seek. Show us the straight way, The way of those on whom Thou hast bestowed Thy

Grace, those whose (portion) is not wrath, and who go not astray.

Adherents of the HANAFI MADH-HAB recite the THANAA after the first TAKBIR instead of the FAATIHAH:

Subhaanakal-lah humma wa bi-himdika * wa tabaa-rakas-muka * wa ta-'aalaa jadduka * wa jalla thanaa-uka * wa laa ilaa-ha ghai-ruk.

Glory to Thee, O Allah! And Thine is the praise. Blessed is Thy name and exalted is Thy majesty. Sublime is Thy praise and there is none to be served besides Thee.

9. The SECOND TAKBIR is pronounced, and the hands are raised to the ears:

Allahu Akbar!
Allah is Greatest!

10. The complete SALAWAAT is then recited:

Allah-humma salli 'alaa sai-yidinaa muham-madin wa alaa aali sai-yidi- naa muhammad

* kammaa sallaita ' alaa sai-yidi-naa ibraa-heema wa 'alaa aali sai-yidinaa ibraaheem * wa barrik 'alaa saiyidinaa muhammadin wa 'alaa aali saiyidinaa muhammad * ka-maa baarakta 'alaa sai-yidinaa ibraaheema wa 'alaa aali saiyidinaa ibraaheema fil 'aalam-een * innaka hameedum majeed.

O Allah! Shower salutations upon our Leader Muhammad and upon the family of our Leader Muhammad as Thou hast showered salutations upon our Leader Ibrahim and upon the family of our Leader Ibrahim. (O Allah!) Shower blessings upon our Leader Muhammad and upon the family of our Leader Muhammad as Thou hast showered blessings upon our Leader Ibrahim and the family of our Leader Ibrahim. Behold, in the entire Universe Thou art surely the Praise-worthy, the Glorious.

[The HANAFIS also utter the second TAKBIR but do not raise their hands after this TAKBIR nor in the subsequent ones. Thereafter they also recite the SALAWAAT. After the third TAKBIR they also repeat a DU'AA for the repose and forgiveness of the deceased; and after the fourth they also give the SALAAM.]

11. Pronounce the THIRD TAKBIR in the usual manner:

ALLAAHU AKBAR

[ALLAH IS THE GREATEST]

12. Recite a Du'aa for the repose and forgiveness of the deceased. Different forms of this Du'aa are reported to have been offered by the Holy Prophet [S]. The following are the most well-known:

DU'AA FOR AN ADULT MUSLIM

ALLAAHUM-MAGH-FIR LI HAYYINAA WA MAYYITINAA, WA SHAAHIDINAA WA GHAA-IBINAA, WA SA-GHIIRINAA WA KABIIRINAA, WA DHA-KARINAA WA UN-THAA-NAA, ALLAAHUMMA MAN AHYAY-

TAHUU MINNAA FA AHYIHII
'ALAL ISLAAM, WA MAN TA-
WAF-FAYTAHUU MINNAA FA
TAWAF-FAHUU 'ALAL II-
MAAN.

13. Pronounce the FOURTH TAKBIIR in the usual manner:

ALLAAHU AKBAR   [ALLAH
IS THE GREATEST]

14. The following Du'aa is then recited:
ALLAAHUMMA LAA TAHRIM-
NAA AJRAHUU (HAA), WA
LAA TAFTINNAA BA'DAHUU
(HAA) WAGH-FIR LANAA WA
LAHUU (HAA) WA LIL MUS-
LIMIIN AJMA'IIN.

15. Finally the TASLIIM is pronounced while the head is turned to the right first, and then to the left.

AS-SALAAMU 'ALAYKUM WA RAHMATUL-

LAAH AS-SALAAMU 'ALAYKUM WA RAHMA-
TULLAAH

Peace and blessings (mercy) of Allah be upon you.

WHAT TO DO IF THE IMAAM ERRS IN THE NUMBER OF TAKBIRS

As explained above, it is a RUKN of the
JANAAZAH Prayer to pronounce four TAK-
BIRS. If the Imaam pronounces one or two
TAKBIRS in addition to the four TAKBIRS the
MA'MOOM should either:

a)   resolve in his mind (NIYYAH) to release
     himself from following the Imaam and give
     the SALAAM, or better still

b)   wait for the Imaam and give the SALAAM after
     him.

In both cases the SALAAH would be in order for
both the Imaam and the followers.

If the Imaam performs three or more TAKBIRS
in addition to the required four, then the

SALAAH is rendered invalid (BAATIL) both for the Imaam and for those who wait for him.

If the Imaam inadvertently performs fewer than four TAKBIRS and realizes his mistake after the SALAAM, he should perform the TAKBIR he has missed immediately. There is no SUJOOD-US-SAHWI in the SALAAT-UL-JANAAZAH.

WHAT THE MA'MOOM SHOULD DO IF HE MISSES TAKBIRS WITH THE IMAAM

If the MA'MOOM joins the Imaam after the latter has already completed one or more TAKBIRS, then he should enter the SALAAH and immediately after his first TAKBIR, recite the FAATI-HAH. If the Imaam performs the following TAKBIR while he is still reciting the FAATIHAH then he should break off his recitation and follow the Imaam who would be carrying his FAATI-HAH. After his second TAKBIR, the follower should recite the SALAWAAT. When the Imaam performs the TASLIM, the follower should perform his third TAKBIR after which he should recite the DU'AA. The fourth TAKBIR should then be performed and the concluding DU'AA made followed by the SALAAM.

If the MA'MOOM joins the JAMAA' late when the Imaam, for instance, performs the second takbir, THEN THE MA'MOOM should perform the TAKBIR with the Imaam and omit the recitation of the FAATIHAH since the Imaam carries his FAATIHAH.

PERSONS FOR WHOM FUNERAL PRAYER IS TO BE PERFORMED

FUNERAL PRAYER FOR A CHILD BORN DEAD

A miscarried fetus, less than four months old, may not be washed (Ghusl), nor may a funeral prayer (Janaazah) be offered for it. It should be wrapped in a piece of cloth and buried. The majority of jurists are in agreement on this point.

On the other hand, if a miscarried fetus is four months or older, and the existence of life in it is established (such as its movements), then there is a consensus that it should be washed and a funeral prayer offered for it. But if its life is not established by its movement or other evidence, then according to Imam Malik, Al-Awzaa'i, Al-Hasan, and the Hanafi school, funeral prayer may not be offered for it. They base their opinion on a hadith transmitted by Imam Tirmidhi, Nasaa-i, Ibn Maajah, and Bayhaqi on the authority of Jaabir that the Prophet, ﷺ, said ;

> *"If in a miscarried fetus life is established by its movements, a funeral prayer should be offered for it, and it is entitled to its share of inheritance."*

According to this hadith offering a funeral prayer for a miscarried fetus is conditional upon proof of its life evident in signs of life, such as its movements, etc.

Imam Ahmad, Sa'iid, Ibn Siriin, and Ishaaq are of the opinion that in light of the above hadith, a miscarried fetus should be washed and a funeral prayer offered for it. The words in this hadith are "a funeral prayer should be offered for a miscaried fetus," because it has a soul and is a. The Prophet, peace be upon him, informed us that a fetus receives a soul when it is four months old.

In another hadith transmitted by Imam Abu Dawuud on the authority of 'Abdullah Ibn 'Umar, the Prophet, ﷺ, said:

> *"Pray on the still-born child, and beg Allah for forgiveness on behalf of its parents." Thus some scholars prescribed Janaazah on all children, regardless of their state at birth.*

A FUNERAL SERVICE OVER A DEAD BODY IN ITS ABSENCE :

SALAAT-UL-GHAA-IB

A funeral service may be held over a dead body in its absence. In other words, if a person had died in another place and has been buried there, then it is allowed for people elsewhere to perform a funeral service over him/her. Instead of the word HAADIR in the IQAAMAH, the word GHAA-IB should be said. Abu Hurairah reported: "The Messenger of Allah ﷺ gave the news of the death of the negus on the day on which he died. He went forth to the place of prayer and made the people stand in ranks and uttered four TAKBIRS."

A FUNERAL SERVICE OVER ONE
WHO HAS COMMITTED SUICIDE

A funeral service shall be offered over a person that has committed suicide. According to one HADITH, the Holy Prophet ﷺ did not lead the funeral service over a man who committed suicide, but his Companions held such a service.

CHAPTER 33

THE BURIAL
THE FOURTH SOCIAL OBLIGATION

The fourth and final social obligation (FARDU KIFAAYAH) we owe to the dead is the burial or DAFN. The deceased should be buried in a grave as soon as possible after the JANAAZAH Prayer.

WHEN A PERSON DIES AT SEA

When a person dies at sea far away from land, all the FARD acts - bathing, shrouding and offering the Funeral Prayer should be observed. The body should then be placed between two planks, and, after a weight is attached to it, cast into the sea.

REQUIREMENTS FOR THE
GRAVE (QABR)

The grave should be dug sufficiently deep to ensure:

a)   that no odour emanates from the body; and

b)   that no wild beasts dig up the body.

To satisfy all requirements the depth of the grave should be approximately two metres and the approximate width one metre. The grave should be long enough for the MAYYIT to lie in and for those laying the MAYYAT inside the grave to get into it (if necessary), and place the MAYYIT in the position as explained below.

TWO TYPES OF GRAVES MAY BE DUG
1. THE LAHD TYPE

Where the soil is hard and firm, a LAHD, i.e., an oblong excavation in the side of the grave, a lateral hollow, the width of the corpse, should be dug on the QIBLAH side for the body to be placed in. Timber or bricks may be used to close the LAHD, so that when the grave is filled with earth the body remains intact.

2. THE SHAQQ TYPE

Where the soil is loose and sandy, a SHAQQ, i.e., a shallow furrow or trench should be dug along the middle of the QABR for the MAYYIT to be placed in. The furrow should be built up with imbaked bricks and some form of cover should be placed over it. (The type of grave differ from place to place and usually the authorities at the cemetary or the Islamic Centre would know what the requirements are.)

HOW TO PLACE THE MAYYIT IN THE QABR

1.   It is desirable that close relatives in the same order of precedence as for the SALAAH, should enter the QABR to place the body in position. The only difference from the order of precedence for leading the SALAAH is that the husband has preference over others

to lower the body of his deceased wife into the grave.

2.   Preferably three persons should enter the grave.

3.   A sheet should be held over the QABR while lowering and burying the MAYYIT, particularly if it is a female.

4.   The MAYYIT should be lowered head first into either type of grave and turned onto its right side to face the QIBLAH.

5.   After the body has been laid in position the bands of cloth at the headside, chest and legside should be untied.

6.   It is SUNNAH for those who positioned the MAYYIT in the grave to recite the following DU'AA:
BISMILLAA-HIR-RAHMAA-NIR-RA-HEEM

WA 'ALAA MILLATTI RASOO-LILLAAHI SALLALLAAHU 'ALAYHI WA SALLAM * AL-LAAHUM-MAFTAH ABWAA-

BAS SAMAA-I LIROOHIHEE (HAA) * WA AKRIM NUZULA-HUU (HAA) * WA WASSI' MADKHALAHUU (HAA) * WA WASSI' LA-HUU (HAA) QAB-RAHUU (HAA).

In the name of Allah, Most Gracious, Most Merciful; and in accordance with the religion of the Messenger of Allah. O Allah! Open the doors of heaven for his (her) soul and let his (her) entrance and abode therein be hon-ourable; and make his (her) grave spacious.

7. Thereafter, spread a handful of soil over the KAFAN.

8. The recess can then be covered with timber. All the openings should be closed with mud or grass. It is SUNNAH to close the recess from the legside for males and from the headside for females.

9. It is SUNNAH for those present to participate in filling the QABR with at least three handfuls of soil.

When throwing the first handful, recite: "MINHAA KHALAQNAAKUM" "From it (the earth) We created thee." When throwing the second handful, recite: "WA FEEHAA NU'EEDUKUM" "And unto it We shall return thee."

When throwing the third handful, recite: "WA MINHAA NUKH-RIJUKUM TAARATAN UKH-RAA" "And from it We shall raise thee a second time."

10. It is SUNNAH to place a stone or piece of timber at the head of the grave for the purpose of locating it.

11. After the burial the first and last RUKU of SURAH BAQARAH may be recited at the headside of the QABR:

﴿ الــم ٥ ذٰلِكَ الكِتَابُ لا رَيْبَ فِيه هُدًى للمُتَّقِينَ ٥ الذِينَ يُؤْمِنُونَ بِالغَيْبِ ويُقِيمُونَ الصَّلاةَ وَمِمَّا رَزَقْنَاهُم يُنْفِقُونَ ٥ والذِينَ يُؤْمِنونَ بِمَا أُنْزِلَ إِلَيْكَ وَمَا أُنْزِلَ مِنْ قَبْلِكَ وَبِالآخِرة هُم يُوقِنُونَ ٥ أُولئك عَلى هُدًى

من رَّبِّهِم وأولئك هم المُفْلِحُونَ ﴾

*Alif-laam-meem * dhaalikal kitaabulaa raibafeehi hudallil-muttaqeen * Alla-dh-eena yu'minoo-na bilghaibi wa yu-qeemoonas salaata wa mimmaa ra-zaq-naa-hum yunfiqoon * walla-dheena yu-e-minoona bi-maa un-zila ilaika wa maa unzila ming qablika wa bil-aakhirati hum yooqinoon * ulaa-ika 'alaa hudam mir rabbi-him * wa ulaa-ika hu-mul muflihoon.*

Alif, Laam, Meem. This is the Book; in it is guidance sure, without doubt, to those who fear Allah; who believe in the Unseen, are steadfast in prayer, and spend out of what We have provided for them; And who believe in the Revelation sent to thee, and sent before thy time, and (in their hearts) have the assurance of the Hereafter. They are on (true) guidance, from their Lord, and it is those who will prosper.

Lillaahi maa fis samaa waati wa maa fil ard *
wa in tubdoo maa fee anfusikum aw tukhfoo-
hu yu haasibkum bi-hil-laa * fa yaghfiru limay
ya-shaa wa yu 'adh-dhiby may ya-shaa *
wallahu 'alaa kulli shai-in qadeer *

Aamanar-rasoolu bi-maa unzila ilaihi mir
rabbi-hee wal mu-e-minoon * kullun aama-
na billaahi wa malaa-ikati- hee wa kutu-bi-
hee wa rusulih * laa mu-farriqu baina ahadim
mir rusulihee wa qaa-loo sa-mi'naa wa ata-
e-naa * ghufraa-naka rabba-naa wa ilaikal
maseer *

Laa yu-kalli-fullahu naf-san illaa wus-'a-haa
* lahaa maa kasabat wa 'alai-haa * lahaa
maa kasabat wa 'alai-haa maktasabat *
rabbanaa laa tu-aa-khidhnaa in-naseena
aw akhta-e-naa * rabbanaa wa laa tahmil
'a-lainaa isran ka-maa ha-malta-hoo 'alal-
ladheena ming qablinaa * rabbanaa wa laa
tu-hammilnaa maa laa taa-qata la-naa bih *
wa'fu 'annaa * wagh-fir la-naa * war ham-
naa * anta maw-laa-naa fansurnaa 'alal
qawmil kaafireen.

To Allah belongeth all that is in the heavens

118

and on earth. Whether ye show what is in your minds or conceal it, Allah calleth you to account for it. He forgiveth whom He pleaseth, and punisheth whom he pleaseth. For Allah hath power over all things. The Apostle believeth in what hath been revealed to him from his Lord, as do the men of faith. Each one (of them) believeth in Allah, His Angels, His books, and His apostles. "We make no distinction (they say) between one and another of His apostles." And they say: "We hear, and we obey: (we seek) Thy forgiveness, our Lord, and to Thee is the end of all journeys."

On no soul doth Allah place a burden greater than it can bear. It gets every good that it earns, and it suffers every ill that it earns. (Pray): "Our Lord! condemn us not if we forget or fall into error; our Lord! lay not on us a burden like that which Thou didst lay on those before us: Our Lord! lay not on us a burden greater than we have strength to bear. Blot our our sins, and grant us forgiveness. Have mercy on us. Thou art our Protector; help us against those who stand against Faith." (2:284-286)

12. Thereafter the TALQEEN, which is as follows, is recited, followed by a DU'AA for the forgiveness of the departed:

THE TALQEEN
THE PROMPTING

In the name of Allah, the Beneficent, the Merciful. There is no deity save Allah. He is alone. He has no partner. Unto Him belongs the sovereignty and to Him belongs all praise; and He is All-Powerful.

﴿ ... لاَ إِلٰهَ إِلَّا هُوَ كُلُّ شَيْءٍ هَالِكٌ إِلَّا وَجْهُهُ لَهُ الْحُكْمُ وَإِلَيْهِ تُرْجَعُونَ ﴾

Everything (that exists) will perish except His own self. To Him belongs the Command, and to Him will be the return of all. (28:88)

﴿ كُلُّ نَفْسٍ ذَائِقَةُ الْمَوْتِ وَإِنَّمَا تُوَفَّوْنَ أُجُورَكُمْ يَوْمَ الْقِيَامَةِ فَمَنْ زُحْزِحَ عَنِ النَّارِ وَأُدْخِلَ الْجَنَّةَ فَقَدْ فَازَ وَمَا الْحَيَاةُ الدُّنْيَا إِلَّا مَتَاعُ الْغُرُورِ ﴾

120

Every soul shall have a taste of death: And only on the Day of Judgement shall you be paid your full recompense. Only he who is saved from the Fire and admitted to the Paradise will have attained the object (of Life): For the life of this world is but goods and chattels of deception. (3:185)

﴿ مِنْهَا خَلَقْنَاكُمْ وِفِيْهَا نُعِيدُكُمْ وِمِنْهَا نُخْرِجُكُمْ تَارَةً أُخْرٰى ﴾

From the (earth) did We create you, And unto it shall We return you, And from it shall We bring you out once again. (20:55)

From the earth did We create you to strive for your rewards, And back to it We return you to decompose and to become dust, And therefore will We resurrect you for the final reckoning.

In the name of Allah; and with Allah; And from Allah and back to Allah; And upon the

121

religion of the Messenger of Allah ﷺ (did you come and go):

﴿ قَالُوا يَا وَيْلَنَا مَنْ بَعَثَنَا مِن مَّرْقَدِنَا هَذَا مَا وَعَدَ الرَّحْمَنُ وَصَدَقَ الْمُرْسَلُونَ ۝ إِن كَانَتْ إِلَّا صَيْحَةً وَاحِدَةً فَإِذَا هُمْ جَمِيعٌ لَدَيْنَا مُحْضَرُونَ ﴾

"This is what (Allah) Most Gracious had promised. And true was the word of the Apostle! It will be no more than a single Blast, when lo! they will all be brought up before us !: (36:52-53)

O servant of Allah, son (daughter) of the servant of Allah, May Allah have mercy on thee. The world and its adornment have departed from you and you now find yourself in one of the partitions of the Last Day. Therefore, forget not the covenant made while departing from the world to the abode of the Hereafter, that is: The attestation that there is none worthy of worship but Allah, and that Muhammad is the Messenger ﷺ of

Allah; And the belief that Paradise is a verity, That hell is a verity, That the questioning in the grave is a verity, That the Doomsday shall come, there being no doubt about it, That Allah will resurrect those who are in the graves.

Know, O servant of Allah! Thou hast accepted Allah as thy Lord, Islam as thy religion, Muhammad as thy Prophet ﷺ, The Quran as thy Guide, the Ka'bah as thy Qiblah, And that all the believers are thy brethren.

O servant of Allah! hold fast to this evidence; And know verily that thou shall remain in this partition until the day of resurrection.

May Allah strengthen thee with the word that stands firm (thrice) O Allah! Strengthen him (her) with the word that stands firm.

﴿ يُثَبِّتُ اللهُ الَّذِينَ ءَامَنُوا بِالقَوْلِ الثَّابِتِ فِي الْحَيَاةِ الدُّنْيَا وَفِي الْآخِرَةِ وَيُضِلُّ اللهُ الظَّالِمِينَ وَيَفْعَلُ مَا يَشَاءُ ﴾

"Allah will establish in strength

those who believe, with the Word
that stands firm, in this world and in
the Hereafter; but Allah will leave,
to stray, those who do wrong: Allah
doeth what He willeth." (14:27)

﴿ يَا أَيَّتُهَا النَّفْسُ الْمُطْمَئِنَّةُ ٥ ارْجِعِي إِلَى
رَبِّكَ رَاضِيةً مَّرْضِيةً ۰ فَادْخُلِي فِي عِبَادِي ٥
وَادْخُلِي جَنَّتِي﴾

(To the righteous soul will be said):
"O (thou) soul, in (complete) rest
and satisfaction! "Come back thou
to thy Lord, Well pleased (thyself),
and well-pleasing unto Him! "Enter
thou, then among my Devotees!
"Yea, enter thou my Heaven!"
(89:27-30)

We appeal to Allah on thy behalf: O Allah! O
One who is close to every lonely person; One
Who is forever present and never absent; Be
a Companion to us in our loneliness, And be
a Companion to him (her) in his (her)
loneliness. Forgive our neighbours and

forgive his neighbours. And inspire him his belief; Tempt us not after him; Forgive us and him and all the Muslims.

Glory to thy Lord! The Lord of Honour and Power. He is free from what they ascribe to Him; And peace unto the Messengers; And praise be to Allah, The Lord and Cherisher of the Universe.

CHAPTER 34

VISITING THE GRAVEYARD

At the beginning of the Holy Prophet's ﷺ mission, visiting the graves was forbidden. The graves were then objects of worship of the pre-Islamic Arabs and was therefore antagonistic to the doctrine of TAWHEED (the Unity of Allah). The Prophet ﷺ later abolished this prohibition and proclaimed the visiting of graves as lawful, provided its object is to remind of the inevitable hour of death, and of the transitory nature of this world and its vanities.

Ibn Masud reported that the Messenger ﷺ of Allah said:

> *"I prohibited you from visiting graves, but visit them now, for surely visiting the graves lessens worldly love, and reminds you of the Hereafter."*

With such an object of view it is SUNNAH MU'AKKADAH to visit the graveyard. If the visit is undertaken with the object of worshipping graves, seeking favour from their inmates, making TAWAAF around the grave or kissing stones or timber or anything else of the grave, then such a visit is HARAAM.

The MAQBARAH could be visited on any day, but is preferable to do so on a Friday.

WHAT TO RECITE ON ENTERING
THE MAQBARAH

It is SUNNAH, on entering the MAQBARAH, to stand facing the graves, and to send salutations to the inmates of the graves and to pray for the forgiveness of the deceased as follows:

Peace by upon you, O ye dwellers in these abodes from among the believers and Muslims. Behold, if Allah wills, we shall meet you. We beseech of Allah safety for us and for you.

WHAT TO RECITE IN THE MAQBARAH

It is Sunnah to recite as much as possible of the Quran and to make DU'AA for the forgiveness of the departed.

According to the HADITH, for example, SURAH FAATIHAH, SURAH IKHLAAS (ch. 112) and SURAH TAKAATHUR (ch. 102) should be recited and thereafter DU'AA should be made for the dead.

It is also related in the HADITH that SURAH YAASEEN be recited once, that SURAH IKHLAAS be recited eleven times. This was the manner the Companions of the Holy Prophet ﷺ visited the MAQBARAH.

CHAPTER 35

THE WAITING PERIOD AND MOURNING OF A WIDOW

THE MEANING OF 'IDDAH

'IDDAH is the period during which it is incumbent upon a woman, whose marriage has been dissolved by divorce or death to abstain from marrying another husband and to remain in seclusion. It is a period of continence imposed on a woman to ascertain if she is pregnant by the husband so as to avoid confusion of the parentage. When a marriage has been dissolved by death there is in addition the consideration of mourning and respect for the deceased husband.

THE DURATION OF THE 'IDDAH

In the case of a marriage dissolved by death either of two types of 'IDDAH may apply:

1. THE 'IDDAH OF A WIDOW WHO IS NOT PREGNANT

*   This type is known as : M'UTADDATUL WAFAA-UL HAA-IL.

*   The duration of this type of 'IDDAH is four months and ten days which is specified by Allah in the Holy Quran:

وَالَّذِينَ يُتَوَفَّوْنَ مِنْكُمْ وَيَذَرُونَ أَزْوَاجًا يَتَرَبَّصْنَ بِأَنْفُسِهِنَّ أَرْبَعَةَ أَشْهُرٍ وَعَشْراً فَإِذَا بَلَغْنَ أَجَلَهُنَّ فَلَا جُنَاحَ عَلَيْكُمْ فِيمَا فَعَلْنَ فِي أَنْفُسِهِنَّ بِالْمَعْرُوفِ وَاللَّهُ بِمَا تَعْمَلُونَ خَبِيرٌ

"Those of you who die, leaving wives, let them keep to themselves for four months and ten days. When they have fulfilled their term, their is no blame on you if they dispose of themselves in a just and reasonable manner. And Allah is well acquainted with what you do."
(SURAH AL-BAQARAH, 2:234)

* The 'IDDAH caused by death commences from the date thereof.

* If the information of death reaches the wife only after the expiry of the period of 'IDDAH, she is not bound to observe 'IDDAH.

* If the husband has divorced his wife by a revocable form of divorce (TALAAQ RAJ'I) and dies while she is still observing 'IDDAH, such an 'IDDAH of DIVORCE will switch to an 'IDDAH of DEATH and she will not be entitled to maintenance (NAFAQAH).

2. THE 'IDDAH OF A WIDOW WHO IS PREGNANT

* This type is known as M'UTADDATUL WAFAA-UL HAAMIL.

* If the woman is pregnant by the husband, the 'IDDAH terminated immediately upon delivery and she may remarry even before he is buried. As regards this type of 'IDDAH Allah says in the Holy Quran:

$$ \text{﴿ وَأُولَاتُ الْأَحْمَالِ أَجَلُهُنَّ أَنْ يَضَعْنَ حَمْلَهُنَّ ﴾} $$

"For those who carry (life within their wombs), their period is until they deliver their burdens." (65:4)

According to Imaam Shafi'i "the 'IDDAH - whether in the case of death or divorce to be fulfilled by (the expiration of) the required months - was intended to (bind) women who are not pregnant; but if they are pregnant the 'IDDAH is dropped."

According to the HANAFI MADH-HAB the 'IDDAH for a pregnant woman lasts for four months and ten days or until delivery, whichever period is longer.

* The 'IDDAH of a pregnant woman terminates subject futo the following conditions:

a) The issue must be related to the deceased husband. If the pregnancy was brought by adultery or fornication (ZINAA) whereupon the person responsible dies, then there is no 'IDDAH on her.

b) In the case of a woman who has committed adultery as a result of which she became pregnant, and her husband dies subsequently, then she is still bound to observe the 'IDDAH of four months and ten days irrespective of whether she gave birth before the expiration of this term.

c) The 'IDDAH only expires upon delivery of all the issue. Where there has to be delivery of twins, for instance, only after delivery of the second child.

d) In the case of a miscarriage, 'IDDAH only expires if the child is formed to some extent. This should be verified by a doctor, a midwife or any such knowledgeable person.

MOURNING (HIDAAD) ON THE DEATH OF A HUSBAND INCUMBENT ON A WIDOW

* Mourning or HIDDAD is incumbent on a woman whose husband has died. She has to observe certain restrictions throughout the duration of her 'IDDAH.

The Prophet ﷺ said:

"It is not lawful for a woman who believes in Allah and Last Day to observe HIDAAD for more than three days on account of the death of any one except her husband; but for him it is incumbent upon her to observe HIDAAD for the term of four months and ten days."

SIGNIFICANCE OF HIDAAD

*   According to Imaam Shafi'i the sole intention of HIDAAD is to signify grief for the decease of a husband who has faithfully adhered to the marriage contract until death. He (Imam Shafi'i) therefore holds that HIDAAD is nor incumbent upon a woman for a husband from whom she is divorced by irrevocable divorce (TALAAQ BAA-IN). Her 'IDDAH remains an 'IDDAH of divorce.

*   According to the HANAFI MADH-HAB, HIDAAD is incumbent as a sign of grief for the loss of the blessings of matrimony, which was not only the means of her support, but also of the preservation of her chastity; and since an irrevocable divorce is a more complete termination of those blessings than even death itself, HIDAAD can in no way be dispensed with in such a circumstance of irrevocable divorce.

* Apart from the manifestation of grief as reason for HIDAAD as mentioned above, there is another reason rendering it incumbent as an essential condition of 'IDDAH. Since marriage to a widow under 'IDDAH is forbidden, she must refrain from adorning or setting off her person by the use of perfume, make-up or sprays, ostentatious clothing or jewellery. The reason for this abstinence is so as not to excite the desires or arouse the interest of men. She should observe the simplest mode of life and abstain from the fineries of this world.

* The widow must confine herself to the house she occupied with her husband at the time of his death. She is not to leave the house to pass her 'IDDAH at the house of even her parents or anywhere else except through necessity such as inability to pay the rent, or fear of thieves or apprehension of the house collapsing.

*   She is allowed to leave the house if there is a dire necessity for her to do so. For example, to go to work for a livelihood for herself and children if there is no other means of providing subsistence; to go to the shop to buy food if there is no one else to do it; to visit sick relatives.

*   She is also allowed, if living alone, to pass the early part of the evening at the house of a neighbour. The major part of the evening should, however, be spent at her house.

PART- III

PHASESOF
EXISTENCE

CHAPTER 36

PHASES OF EXISTENCE

Almighty Allah says in the Qur'an :

$$ \text{﴿ مِنْهَا خَلَقْنَاكُمْ وَفِيهَا نُعِيدُكُمْ وَمِنْهَا نُخْرِجُكُم تَارَةً أُخْرَى ﴾} $$

*From the (earth) did We create you,
and into it shall We return you, and
from it shall We bring you out once
again. (20:55)*

O Mankind! If you have a doubt about the
resurrection, (consider) that We created you out
of dust, then out of sperm, then out of a leech-
like clot, then out of a morsel of flesh, partly
formed and partly unformed, in order that We
may manifest (Our power) to you; and We
cause whom We will to rest in the wombs for an
appointed term, then do We bring you out as
babes, then (foster you) that you may reach
your age of full strength; and some of you are
call to die, and some are sent back to the

feeblest old age, so that they know nothing after having known (much), and (further), they see the earth barren and lifeless, but when We pour down rain on it, it is stirred (to life), it swells, and it puts forth every kind of beautiful growth (in pairs).

This is so , because God is the Reality: it is He Who gives life to the dead, and it is He Who has power over all things.

﴿ وَأَنَّ السَّاعَةَ لَا رَيْبَ فِيهَا وَأَنَّ اللّٰه يَبْعَثُ مَنْ فِي الْقُبُورِ ﴾

And verily the Hour will come: There can be no doubt about it, or about (the fact) that God will raise up all who are in the graves. (22:7)

There are four different forms of life for people to complete their life span. These are:

PHASE ONE :   LIFE IN THE WOMB

PHASE TWO :   LIFE ON EARTH

PHASE THREE :   LIFE IN THE GRAVE

PHASE FOUR :   LIFE IN THE HEREAFTER

Each of these Phases will be discussed in the following chapters.

CHAPTER 37

PHASE ONE : LIFE IN THE WOMB

PHASE ONE. The first life is that in the womb of the mother where the soul is to join the flesh after the zygote is formed. In Surah Al-Ra'd (Thunder) Allah informs us that He knows exactly what every mother bears in her womb, as well as the number of days the foetus is going to stay in his mother's womb. The Qur'an states the following:

$$﴿ اَللّٰهُ يَعْلَمُ مَا تَحْمِلُ كُلُّ أُنْثٰى وَمَا تَغِيضُ الْأَرْحَامُ وَمَا تَزْدَادُ وَكُلُّ شَيْءٍ عِنْدَهُ بِمِقْدَارٍ ﴾$$

"God does know what every female (womb) does bear, by how much the wombs fall short (of their time or number) or do exceed. Every single thing is before His sight in (due) proportion." (13:8)

Allah also informs us that He Himself is the One who shapes us the way He wants in the wombs of our mothers. The Qur'an states the following in Surah Al-'Imran (The Family of Imran):

﴿ هُوَ الَّذِي يُصَوِّرُكُم فِي الْأَرْحَامِ كَيْفَ يَشَاءُ لَا إِلٰهَ إِلَّا هُوَ الْعَزِيزُ الْحَكِيمُ ﴾

"He is it who shapes you in the wombs as He pleases. There is no god but He, The Exalted in Might, The Wise. (3:6)

Allah created people in the wombs of their own mothers with different stages. The foetus is hidden inside three successive layers above each other. In Surah Al-Zumar, (The Crowds), Allah says the following:

﴿ خَلَقَكُم مِن نَفْسٍ وَاحِدَةٍ ثُمَّ جَعَلَ مِنْهَا زَوْجَهَا وَأَنْزَلَ لَكُمْ مِنَ الْأَنْعَامِ ثَمَانِيَةَ أَزْوَاجٍ يَخْلُقُكُمْ فِي بُطُونِ أُمَّهَاتِكُمْ خَلْقًا مِنْ بَعْدِ خَلْقٍ فِي ظُلُمَاتٍ ثَلَاثٍ ذٰلِكُمُ اللهُ رَبُّكُمْ لَهُ الْمُلْكُ لَا إِلٰهَ إِلَّا هُوَ فَأَنَّى تَصْرَفُونَ ﴾

"He created you (all) from a single person: Then created, of like nature, his mate; and He sent down for you

*eight heads of cattle in pairs; He
makes you, in the wombs of your
mothers, in stages, one after another, in three veils of darkness.
Such is God, your Lord and Cherisher: to Him belongs All Sovereignty. There is no god but He: then
how are you turned away (from your
true Lord)? (39:6)*

Allah informs us that He brought us from the
wombs of our mothers while we were unaware
about anything around us. Then He developed
our sight, hearing, thinking, etc. This description
is explained in Surah Al-Nahl (The Bee). Allah
says the following:

﴿ وَاللّٰهُ أَخْرَجَكُم مِّن بُطُونِ أُمَّهَاتِكُمْ لَا
تَعْلَمُونَ شَيْئًا وَجَعَلَ لَكُمُ السَّمْعَ وَالْأَبْصَارَ
وَالْأَفْئِدَةَ لَعَلَّكُمْ تَشْكُرُونَ ﴾

*"It is He Who brought you forth from
the wombs of your mothers when you
knew nothing; and He gave you*

hearing and sight and intelligence and affections: That you may give thanks (to God). (16:78)

Finally, the Qur'an is very explicit about the creation of man through the process of fertilization, the formation of the zygote and the series of biological, physiological and spiritual developments that take place in the wombs of mothers. In Surah Al-Hajj (The Pilgrimage), Allah describes the whole process of the four types and forms of life that a person has to go through. The Qur'an states the following:

"O Mankind! If you have a doubt about the resurrection, (consider) that We created you out of dust, then out of sperm, then out of a leech-like clot, then out of a morsel of flesh, partly formed and partly unformed, in order that We may manifest (Our power) to you; and We cause whom We will to rest in the wombs for an appointed term,

then do We bring you out as babes, then (foster you) that you may reach your age of full strength; and some of you are call to die, and some are sent back to the feeblest old age, so that they know nothing after having known (much), and (further), they see the earth barren and lifeless, but when We pour down rain on it, it is stirred (to life), it swells, and it puts forth every kind of beautifulgrowth (in pairs).

This is so , because God is the Reality: it is He Who gives life to the dead, and it is He Who has power over all things.

﴿ وَأَنَّ السَّاعَةَ لَا رَيْبَ فِيهَا وَأَنَّ اللهَ يَبْعَثُ مَنْ فِي الْقُبُورِ ﴾

And verily the Hour will come: There can be no doubt about it, or about (the fact) that God will raise up all who are in the graves. (22:5-7)

145

CHAPTER 38
PHASE TWO : LIFE ON EARTH

PHASE TWO. The second phase of life is the one we are living here on this planet where the flesh and the soul are united and are working together in unison.

However, it should be stated here that life on this planet is short and temporary. It is one of the segments of the life span of mankind that they have to go through. It is not eternal. it is a life of tests and examinations; a life of enjoyment and entertainment; and a life of rewards and turmoil. It is a life of preparation for the following life to come. One has to make sure to leave at anytime without his knowledge or even without his permission, If one thinks that there is no more life to live after this life, it is to his disadvantage and to this discontentment.

At the same time it may be too awful to live. One may say that there is no need for us to live on this planet this short period of life. The only logical way is to think, to recognize and to believe the there should be a life to come after this life. And that is the real life.

CHAPTER 39

PHASE THREE : LIFE IN THE GRAVE

PHASE THREE. The third phase of life is that of the grave, where the soul and flesh are separated from one another. The flesh goes into the soil and is catabolized back to its original sources, namely: silicon, magnesium, calcium, potassium, phosphorus, sulfur, nitrogen, carbon dioxide, energy, and water. However, the soul is taken to Isthmus (Al-Barzakh), and is stored there until the Day of Judgement. Although, there will be frequent visitation of the soul to the grave for reward or punishment.

CHAPTER 40
PHASE FOUR : LIFE IN
THE HEREAFTER

PHASE FOUR. The fourth phase of life is the one in the hereafter, which starts with the blowing of the trumpet or horn. People are to be resurrected from their graves through their own embryos, namely, the 'Ajaf of the sacrum. Then there will be the Assembly and Judgement which are followed by Hell and Paradise; or people are to be stationed among the waiting lists in the areas of A'raaf.

All these phases of life will also be discussed in greater detail in the following pages.

It should be stated here that the first three phases of life have definite life span and definite number of days, months, and years. The fourth phase of life (The hereafter) is an eternal one. There is no retreat and there is no way that a person will be able to come back to this life. Hence, one has to make use of the life span on this planed before it is too late for him. Ons should prepare himself long in advance in every aspect of life: spiritually, socially, economically, psychology, and with good intention.

CHAPTER 41

REFLECTIONS ON THE

JOURNEY OF THE SOUL

INTRODUCTION

It is understood that our root was in Heaven where Adam and Eve were living. They were the first human beings who landed on this earth. It is also understood that we are their children. We carry the good (and the bad) traits on the chromosomes of our reproductive cells, namely, the physical, the biological, the chemical, and to a certain extent the behavioral activities.

PHASE 1: LIFE IN THE WOMB

When conception takes place, fertilization produces the zygote of the individual. After forty days the soul is blown into the flesh to become a human being. The person has to live about nine months as a fetus in the womb of his mother. After which he has to come out as a male or a female. He has no choice to decide whether he should come to this world or not. He has no choice to decide whether he should be born as a boy or as a girl. He has no choice to decide who are his parents. He has no choice to decide to be born black, white, brown, or albino. he has no choice to be born in America, Europe, Africa, Asia, or other areas. Allah of these points and many more are beyond his control.

PHASE 2: LIFE ON THIS PLANET

After being born, his personality is affected by genetics, foods, society, and hidayah (Guidance) from God. He is given the choice to decide after the age of puberty as to which way he wished to follow. Hence, he will be charged or rewarded accordingly.

The person may live a few seconds or as long as 140 years or more. During this phase of his life, the soul and the flesh are working together, stay together except at sleeping where the soul departs the flesh temporary or forever. Qur'an stated emphatically the departure of the soul at sleeping in Surah Al-Zumar (The Crowds):

﴿ اللهُ يَتَوَفَّى الْأَنْفُسَ حِيْنَ مَوْتِهَا وَالَّتِي لَمْ تَمُتْ فِي مَنَامِهَا فَيُمْسِكُ الَّتِي قَضَى عَلَيْهَا الْمَوْتَ وَيُرْسِلُ الْأُخْرَى إِلَى أَجَلٍ مُسَمَّى إِنَّ فِي ذَلِكَ لَآيَاتٍ لِقَوْمٍ يَتَفَكَّرُونَ ﴾

"It is God that takes The souls (of men) at death; And those that die not (He takes) during their sleep: Those on whom He Has passed the decree of death, He keeps back (From returning to Life), but the rest He sends (To their bodies) For a term appointed. Verily in this are Signs For those who reflect... (39:42)

During this phase of life, there are continuous biological processes of life and death. In every cell, organ, system of organs, life is being produced, and death is being rendered. Allah creates life from death, and He does produce death from life. The Qur'an states these processes emphatically. In Surah Al-Imran

151

Allah says the following:

﴿ تُولِجُ اللَّيْلَ فِي النَّهَارِ وَتُولِجُ النَّهَارَ فِي اللَّيْلِ وَتُخْرِجُ الْحَيَّ مِنَ الْمَيِّتِ وَتُخْرِجُ الْمَيِّتَ مِنَ الْحَيِّ وَتَرْزُقُ مَنْ تَشَاءُ بِغَيْرِ حِسَابٍ ﴾

"You caused the Night to gain on the Day, and you caused the Day to gain on the Night; you bring the Living Out of the Dead, and you bring the Dead out of the Living; and you give sustenance to whom you please, without measure." (3:27)

Therefore, there are hundreds of thousands of enzymatic reactions that take place in the body every fraction of a second. Some of which are used in the process of anabolism to build up and to synthesize new materials, while others are being used to catabolize the biological entities of the body. Some of these biochemical reactions are utilized to synthesize living materials while others are either to synthesize dead materials or to get rid of living materials.

This second phase of life will cease completely

when the soul is taken away from the flesh. At the time, the person is to go to his third phase of his life. he has no choice as to when he is to depart this world, or even how to leave it. If he is smart, he plans himself will in advance. Nothing goes with him. He is to leave everything behind him. The only thing that goes with him are his deeds, preceded by his intention.

PHASE 3: LIFE IN THE GRAVE

This third phase of life is considered to be life in the grave. This type of life is one where the soul and flesh have been separated completely from being one biological entity. It is understood that the biological entity of the person is to be catabolized, fermented, decayed, autolysed, degraded and finally to become carbon dioxide, water, energy, oxygen, and nitrogen. While the inorganic entity will become silicon, calcium, magnesium, sulfur, sodium, etc.

There will remain only the seed and its embryo, namely the 'Ajaf of the Sacrum. During the process of dormancy, the seed is to be prepared for the new life to come. Many processes take place including physiological, physical, meta-bolic, metamorphic, and others. It stays there till the Day of Judgement.

Since the soul is to stay in Isthmus, it will visit the grave regularly for rewards or punishments. One has to recognize that life in the grave is either part of Paradise or a ditch in Hell.

PHASE 4: THE HEREAFTER

SUBPHASE 4.1: REBIRTH (RESURRECTION)

This phase starts with a series of incidents that have to take place in order that the embryos of the seeds of human beings will germinate. Then the new life starts. After dormancy, and at time of rebirth, Allah instructs Angel Israafeel to blow the trumpet twice. The first one is to shake up every seed to be ready for germination. Water of life is to pour upon the seeds in graves. The soul comes back from Isthmus to join its entity. The second blow of the trumpet will help seeds to germinate and to produce eveperson. They come out of their graves in a state of shock. They will come out clotheless and shoeless.

Every one has to come out exactly with the same identification features. The finger prints will be exactly the same. Their DNA and RNA will be exactly the same. There will not be any confusion at all as to the identity of each person.

SUBPHASE 4.2: ASSEMBLY DAY

Each person is to be brought to a place of Assembly. All swill be waiting for the Court of Allah, the Court of Justice to decide for them. That Day of Assembly is a day of agony, anxiety, and a day of worries. It is a day where everyone is to worry about himself. No one has the time to worry about others.

With the heat of sun, with the sweating, and with the presence of too many people next to one another, the dilemma is too much to be accepted or to be experienced. Each one is worried what is going to happen to him personally. However, some seven groups of people are to be protected by Allah when He exalts Himself upon them.

Since it is the Assembly Day, each is to be grouped after his leader, prophet, messenger, mentor, celebrity, and the like. All will be put in lines waiting for the Court of Allah to take place.

SUBPHASE 4.3: JUDGEMENT DAY

This is the Day where everyone personally is to be judged by Allah directly with absolute justice. There will not be any bias or prejudice. Each one will be able to receive his Book in his right or left hand according to his achievements. In that Book he will be able to find out each and every item he has made from the time of birth till the time of death. The Book includes activities, appearance and intention. Such a Book could be similar to a video tape which records all these three parameters.

That is the Day where some people are to be happy, excited, surprised and grateful to God for His Mercy, Blessings, Forgiveness, Graciousness and as being accepted by God. This group of people are the ones who are to receive their Book in their right hands.

The other group of people are those who will be unfortunate. Their faces express gloom. They are distressed with anxiety and worries. They wish that life will be generated again on this planet to do the good instead the bad things. They are the ones who are to receive their Book in their left hands.

SUBPHASE 4.4: LIFE IN HELL

This phase of life is the place where ever body is to zoom towards a place and to be visited. Is Life in Hell. Some people are to be saved from being dumped into it. Others would be taken to another station called Al-A'raf. They don't deserve to enter Paradise; and the Mercy of Allah does not allow them to enter Hell. There is a group of people who do deserve to enter Hell. They are either to stay for a short period of time to be purified or to stay forever.

SUBPHASE 4.5: LIFE IN PARADISE

This phase of life is the last but not the least. It is the most important phase of life for human beings to go to, to live in, to experience and to enjoy. It is the aim and hope of every person to go there. It is the root of life for Adam and Eve, where they lived there and enjoyed it.

That life is an eternal one. It has all the beauties of life to enjoy without being tired, or exhausted. It is a life of excitement, peace, happiness, and concord. It is the life without hate, jealousy, cheating, lying, or any other vices. It is a place where matrimonial life does exist without the agony or diseases. This is the Real and the True Life.

REFERENCES

* 'ALI, ALLAMA 'ABDULLAH YUSUF, THE HOLY QUR'AN: TRANSLATION AND COMMENTARY, (U.S.A.: AMERICAN TRUST PUBLICATIONS, 1977).

* PICKTHALL, MOHAMMAD MARMADUKE, THE GLORIOUS QUR'AN, (KARACHI:TAJ COMPANY LTD.).

* MAWDUDI, SAYYID ABUL A'LA, THE MEANING OF THE QUR'AN, (LAHORE: ISLAMIC PUBLICATIONS LIMITED, 1987).

* DR. TAQUDIN HALALI AND DR. MUHSAN KHAN "THE NOBLE QURAN' SAUDI ARABIA.

* IBN KATHEER, TAFSEER AL-QUR'AN AL-AZEEM, (BEIRUT: DAR AL-KUTUB AL-'IL-MIYYAH, 1st ED., 1986).

* IMAM AL-QURTUBI, TAFSEER AL-QURTUBI.

* IMAM AL-BUKHARI, SAHIH AL-BUKHARI: ENGLISH TRANSLATION BY DR. MUHAMMAD MUHSIN KHAN, (PAKISTAN, 1971). * AL-ASQALAANI, AL-HAAFIZ IBN HAJAR: FAT-HUL BAARI BI SHARH SAHIIH AL-BUKHARI. * IMAM MUSLIM, SAHIH MUSLIM: TRANSLATED BY 'ABDUL HAMEED SIDDIQI, (LAHORE: SH. MUHAMMAD ASHRAF, 1981). * IMAM NAWAWI, SHARH SAHIIH MUSLIM.

* AL-GHAZALI, IMAM ABU HAMID, IHYAA

'ULOOM AD-DEEN, (DAR AL-MAKTAB AL-'ARABIYYAH). * SAKR, AHMAD H., LIFE, DEATH AND THE LIFE HEREAFTER, (U.S.A., FOUNDATION FOR ISLAMIC KNOWLEDGE, 1992).

* IBN AL-QAYYIM, AL-IMAM IBN AL-QAYYIM AL-JAWZIYYAH, KITAAB AR-ROOH, TRANS-LATED BY A. BEWLEY, (LONDON: DAR AL-TAQWA LTD., 1987).

* FAKIR, SHEIKH ABU BAKR, MANUAL OF PRAYER AND FASTING, (SOUTH AFRICA, 1987).

* KUTTY, AHMAD, ISLAMIC FUNERAL RITES AND PRACTICES, (TORONTO: ISLAMIC FOUN-DATION OF TORONTO, 1991).

* HAMID, SHEIKH 'ABDUL WAHID, ISLAM THE NATURAL WAY, (LONDON: MELS, 1989).

* KASIM, DR. MUNIR, A MATTER OF LIFE AND DEAT

THE BOOKS WE PUBLISHED

* The Bible Led me to Islam.	Abdul-Malik LeBlanc
* A Guide for Hajj and Umrah.	Anis & Daud Matthews
* Why Islam is Our Only Choice?	M. Hanif Shahid
* What God Said About Eating Pork?	Shabir Ally
* Common Questions People Ask About Islam.	Shabir Ally
* Science in the Qur'an.	Shabir Ally
* Is Jesus god? the Bible says - No.	Shabir Ally
* 101 Questions People ask Visiting Jehovah's Witnesses.	Shabir Ally
* 101 Clear Contradictions in the Bible.	Shabir Ally
* Source of Islamic Theories.	Shabir Ally
* Follow Jesus Or Follow Paul?	Dr. Roshan Inaam
* Decision of the Court : Qadianies are not Muslims	Muhammad Bashir M.A.
* Forty Hadith (English)	Imam Al-Nawawi
* Islamic Guidelines	Muhammad Jamil Zino
* What a Muslim Believes?	Muhammad Jamil Zino
* Pillars of Islam and Iman	Muhammad Jamil Zino
* Islamic Creed based on Qur'an and Sunnah	Muhammad Jamil Zino
* Islamic Creed (Spanish).	Muhammad Jamil Zino
* The Universe Seen Through the Qur'an.	Dr. Mir Anees uddin, Ph,d.
* Help Your Self in Reading The Qura'n.	Sheikh Faisal Abdul Razaq
* Actions are by Intention.	Sheikh Faisal Abdul Razaq
* The Book of Death.	Sheikh Faisal Abdul Razaq
* Pearl of the Truth on the Beautiful Names of Allah.	Sheikh Sidheeque M.A.
* Doomsday: Portents & Prophecies.	Sheikh Sidheeque M.A.
* Vital Herald to Pilgrims.	Sheikh Sidheeque M.A.
* Monotheism & Pantheism.	Amir Hamza

URDU PUBLICATIONS	
* Shab - O - Roze Ki Duaeen (Fortification) Urdu Pocket Size.	Sheikh Abdullah Jar Allah
* Hajj and Umrah Urdu Pocket Size.	Sheikh Abdul Aziz Bin Baz
* Siyasi aur Mazhabi Baway.	Amir Hamza
* Allah Majood Nahin?.	Amir Hamza
* Shaar'a-e-Bahisht.	Amir Hamza
* Aasmani Jannat aur Darbari Jahannam.	Amir Hamza
* Maout ke Farishtay say Mulaqat.	Amir Hamza
* Baran-e- Tauheed.	Amir Hamza
ARABIC PUBLICATIONS	
* Kitab al-Tohid (Arabic).	Sheikh Abdul Wahab
* Forty Hadith (Arabic) Pocket Size.	Imam Al-Nawawi
* Doomsday Portents & Prophecies in Arabic.	Izzuddin Hosain Al-Sheikh